YORK NOTES

General Editors: Professor A.N. Jeffares (*University of Stirling*) & Professor Suheil Bushrui (*American University of Beirut*)

Wilfred Owen

SELECTED POEMS

Notes by Benedikte Uttenthal

MA (CAMBRIDGE) MA (ESSEX)

LONGMAN
YORK PRESS

YORK PRESS
Immeuble Esseily, Place Riad Solh, Beirut.

LONGMAN GROUP LIMITED
Longman House,
Burnt Mill,
Harlow,
Essex

First published 1986
ISBN 0 582 79287 8
Produced by Longman Group (FE) Ltd.
Printed in Hong Kong

Contents

Part 1

Introduction

The life of Wilfred Owen

Wilfred Owen died at the age of twenty-five, killed in action only seven days before the end of the First World War. He had written some hundred and ten poems, numerous poetic fragments and slightly less than seven hundred letters. His complete writings fill no more than three volumes. He died tragically young and his poetic work remained youthful. He is, however, regarded as the outstanding English poet of the First World War. This not an undeserved reputation, but it can be misleading as Wilfred Owen was already an inspired apprentice poet before the war began. The war alone did not make him; he made war a poetic subject. It is the business of these Notes to see how this came about, as well as to explore the other themes of his poetry.

Wilfred Owen was the eldest of four children and had been born into seemingly prosperous circumstances on 18 March 1893. His birth-place, Oswestry, Shropshire, was the home of his maternal grandfather, a small businessman, with whom his parents were living. At the grandfather's death in 1897 it was discovered that he had been living off his capital and that there was almost nothing left for his heirs. The comfortable house and leisurely life were now beyond the Owen family's means and for the next ten years, until Wilfred was in his early teens, they lived very modestly in the poorer districts of Birkenhead. This was where Wilfred's father, Tom, worked with the railway companies, holding posts of responsibility that were, however, poorly paid. He worked there out of necessity only, cherishing as an escape a love of music and a love of the sea. He, and particularly his wife Susan, inspired by memories of their happier days at Oswestry, struggled against poverty to maintain standards of speech, dress and behaviour. Their struggle isolated them from their neighbours (dockers and stevedores) and drew them closer together. Susan Owen, a little disappointed in her husband's ability to provide for herself and the children, concentrated most of her affections and hopes on her eldest son, Wilfred. He, in turn, adored her. On the evidence of his letters to her, as well as of his poetry, it is clear that her somewhat jealous attentiveness had a profound effect on his emotional development, increasing his responsiveness in certain areas while severely stunting it in others.

If Wilfred was Susan's favourite, Harold, their second son (born in

1897, two years after their daughter Mary), was Tom's favourite. Harold Owen was to publish a three-volume biography of the Owen family, cumbersomely but not inaccurately entitled *Journey from Obscurity: Wilfred Owen 1893–1918: Memoirs of the Owen Family.** These three volumes give a vivid and compassionate account not only of Wilfred as seen from Harold's point of view, but of the Owen's close-knit family life and of Harold's own frustrated career as a painter, deflected by his father and lack of funds into the Merchant Navy and later during the First World War into the Royal Navy. Colin Owen, the fourth and last child, was born in 1900.

Wilfred was already known as a 'swot' in the Junior School of the Birkenhead Institute where he was sent by his parents in 1899, his interests being imaginative and literary rather than physically active or convivial. The restricted circumstances of their Birkenhead days were sometimes alleviated by holidays in Ireland or the English countryside, and there were friends and relatives to add variety. Memories of Oswestry, however, continued to fuel Susan's genteel ambitions and to work as a reproach on Tom. The family became emotionally split: Susan and her eldest, Wilfred, being on one side, Tom and the other three children on the other. Of the total 673 letters of Wilfred Owen, found and edited by Harold Owen and John Bell,† 554 were written in obvious devotion to his mother, while only five were addressed to his father.

It was on a holiday at Broxton in the summer of 1903 or 1904, the greater part of it spent alone with his mother, that 'the poetry in Wilfred, with gentle pushings, without hurt, began to bud, and not on the battlefields of France'.**

> For I fared back into my life's arrears
> Even the weeks at Broxton, by the Hill,
> Where first I felt my boyhood fill
> With uncontainable movements; there was born
> My poethood.‡

In 1907 Tom found a better post with the railways and the Owen family moved to Shrewsbury. Wilfred eventually attended the Shrewsbury Technical School, working hard in his attic bedroom and developing an interest in religion. His mother was ardently religious and he was ardent in trying to please her. Susan Owen was an evangelical Anglican, that is to say, she believed in redemption through faith rather than

---

* Oxford University Press, London, 1963–5.
† *Wilfred Owen: Collected Letters*, Oxford University Press, London, 1967.
** Harold Owen, *Journey from Obscurity: Wilfred Owen 1893–1918*, Oxford University Press, London, 1963, Vol. 1, p.103.
‡ Wilfred Owen, *The complete poems and fragments*, ed. Jon Stallworthy, Chatto & Windus, London, 1983, Vol. II, p.433.

through good deeds. It was a fatalistic faith and one that required self-sacrifice and passivity. Its style was more part of her character than a necessary part of evangelicalism. Wilfred Owen's attitude towards this style of worship and these qualities of his mother's was to become ambivalent when he started to live away from home (for the first time in 1911), but in his earlier years he absorbed them uncritically. Here was a source for the themes of ritual, self-sacrifice, divine and maternal love that were to occur in his poetry.

But he had other interests too. With his cousins he formed an Astronomical, Geological and Botanical Society. He developed an interest in archaeology which was to bear poetic fruit in his 1913 poem 'Uriconium: An Ode'. And by now he was reading William Wordsworth (1770–1850), John Keats (1795–1821) and Percy Bysshe Shelley (1792–1822).

It is not known when Wilfred Owen started to write poetry. He left strict instructions with his mother to burn a sack of papers—which contained no doubt the answer to this question—should he die in the war, and these instructions were faithfully carried out at his untimely death in 1918. His earliest surviving poem is probably 'To Poesy', written in 1909–10. This is heavily indebted to Keats whom Wilfred almost worshipped. Throughout his short life his predominant taste in poetic reading were the Romantic and Victorian writers. He was unaware of the poetry of Ezra Pound (1885–1972), of the other imagists, of T.S. Eliot's (1888–1965) first volume of verse, published in 1917, and of the W.B. Yeats (1865–1939) of *The Green Helmet* (1910) and *Responsibilities* (1914). As well as Keats and Shelley, he read John Ruskin (1819–1900), Alfred Tennyson (1809–92), Elizabeth Barrett Browning (1806–61), and Algenon Charles Swinburne (1837–1909), all of whom were to influence him greatly. Most obviously they helped to develop his sensuous vision and his ability to apply it to the unpleasant as well as the pleasant. Shelley had written in his *A Defence of Poetry*, 'Poetry turns all things to loveliness; it exalts the beauty of that which is most beautiful, and it adds beauty to that which is most deformed; it marries exultation and horror, grief and pleasure, eternity and change.* This reads like a prescription for Owen's war poetry. These nineteenth-century writers were also behind his aestheticising attitude, his cult of beauty which nevertheless moved towards the great empathy he could feel with his subjects. This empathy had been discussed and defined by Keats as 'negative capability' in a famous letter of his to George and Tom Keats (21, 27 (?) December 1817). Owen's letter to his mother from Craiglockhart (8 August 1917) † is an example of Keats' 'negative

---

* Quoted in *English Critical Texts* ed. D.J. Enright and E. De Chickera, Oxford University Press, London, 1962, p.252.
† *Collected Letters*, p.408.

capability' put into practice (see Part 2, p.30). He shared the Romantic poets' view of the inadequacy of the existing world, and of the need to create a finer world both in poetry and through poetry. With Shelley and with Ruskin he was to see a moral aspect in art, one that could have an effect upon society. But as well as all these qualities, he would share with them the view that being a poet meant suffering and isolation, that he would become the lone meteor of his poem 'O World of many Worlds'.

Leaving home: Dunsden

When Wilfred Owen was eighteen and had left school, he tried a spell as a pupil teacher, but found it prevented him from studying for the university entrance examination. He passed the University of London matriculation examination in September 1911, but not with high enough marks to gain the scholarship he desperately needed, as his parents were unable to provide the necessary money for fees and living expenses. It was on the understanding that coaching and time for private study would be given in return for help with parish work that he became an assistant to the Reverend Herbert Wigan in the parish of Dunsden, Oxfordshire, in October of that year.

His time at Dunsden was a mixed blessing. The Vicar did not help him much with his studies and he felt robbed of time for his private interests by his numerous parish duties. The hypocrisies and inadequacies of organised religion became apparent to him and his childhood faith was undermined. But he was learning to be independent and form views of his own. He decided that he would not be able to sacrifice his love of poetry and respect for scientific knowledge which he felt it his duty to do if he were to become an evangelical minister.

It is one of the marked characteristics of his writing that he felt unable to reconcile the interests of art and religion. He created a dichotomy on a half-realised notion that art was based on sensuality which was at least potentially, if not inherently, evil while religion should be entirely separate from the needs of the flesh. It seems an inevitable product of his mother's puritanical jealousy and his romantic readings and preoccupations. The dichotomy and its gradual resolution are well illustrated by the 'Maundy Thursday' sonnet:

Then I too knelt before the acolyte.
Above the crucifix I bent my head:
The Christ was thin, and cold, and very dead:
And yet I bowed, yea, kissed—my lips did cling
(I kissed the warm live hand that held the thing).
(probably drafted May/June 1915)

At Dunsden he continued his studies in botany and literature with the help of tutors at University College Reading, and on their advice he read Ruskin and John Milton (1608–74). He wrote around a dozen poems, two of which were lengthy narratives based on the Danish writer Hans Christian Andersen's (1805–75) fairy tales 'Little Claus and Big Claus' and 'The Little Mermaid', the latter a competent piece in the Keatsian vein. This set of poems reveals that he was leading a double life: he was writing in his spare time verse quite unconnected with, and indeed unconformable to, his respectably maintained front as a prospective churchman. This, and the fact that he was abandoning the faith of his mother, put him under a great deal of emotional stress. He left Dunsden early in 1912 in somewhat obscure circumstances (the crucial letter having been censored by his brother Harold), but obviously because of his lack of religious convictions and perhaps also because the vicar disapproved of some 'friendship' in the parish—though it should not be supposed that there had been any serious scandal. From that period, there are erotic and homosexually tinged poems in which he celebrates the beauty of the human body—usually the male body. This is, however, a not uncommon recourse of repressed and puritanically educated youth, where physical admiration of the same sex can be seen as free from sin. These poems should not therefore be read as clear evidence of homosexuality. He was, however, under the influence of his mother who greatly discouraged him from taking an interest in women, and he never really outgrew this influence before his death.

Though he was relieved to depart from Dunsden, he was also much distressed. His future was again insecure and there was less hope than ever of his gaining a scholarship to university. He became quite ill, and not merely physically. In his letters during this period there are a few references to a mental agitation and sleeplessness, including 'phantasies' (2 November 1913), which can be seen as foreshadowing his susceptibilities to the shell-shock that was to hit him in 1917. Later in 1912 he tried to win a scholarship to Reading University and failed. This marked the end of his university aspirations.

France

He went instead to Bordeaux as a teacher of English at the Berlitz School in September 1913. There he perfected his French, though the long hours of work again left him little time for his own pursuits. In July 1914 he was offered the post of tutor in the High Pyrenees to a well-off and friendly family, the Legers. This post he gladly accepted. He was able to write again, and met his first well-known literary figure, the elderly symbolist poet and pacifist Laurent Tailhade (1854–1919) who gave him affection and encouragement. (All the influential literary figures that Owen was to meet were decriers of the war.) He wrote several poems during this period, though few can be dated with any certainty. Some poems revised later at Craiglockhart War Hospital, Edinburgh, or at Scarborough during 1917 were certainly inspired by his experiences during his period in France as a private tutor. Most obvious of these are: 'Maundy Thursday'; 'To —'; '1914'; 'From My Diary, July 1914'; 'The Sleeping Beauty'; and possibly also 'The One Remains' and 'The city lights along the waterside'.

Great Britain joined in the war on 4 August 1914, when Wilfred Owen was still with the Legers in France. Recruiting in Britain was on a voluntary basis until 1916. Wilfred Owen's initial reaction to the war was a posture: one of conventional romantic patriotism, comparable to that sustained by Rupert Brooke (1887–1915) until his death. Brooke, however, as Owen at that time, had seen little of the horrors of war. A brief extract will illustrate Owen's attitude then:

> O meet it is and passing sweet
> To live in peace with others,
> But sweeter still and far more meet
> To die in war for brothers.*

But Owen was in no hurry to join up. It is striking that, in his letters, the war scarcely merited a mention between its outbreak and the spring of 1915. On 28 August 1914 he wrote to his mother:

> I feel my own life all the more precious and more dear in the pre-
> sence of this deflowering of Europe. While it is true that the guns
> will effect a little useful weeding, I am furious with chagrin to think
> that the minds which were to have excelled the civilization of ten
> thousand years, are being annihilated—and bodies, the product of
> aeons of Natural Selection, melted down to pay for political statues.
> I regret the mortality of the English regulars less than that of French,
> Belgian, or even Russian or German armies: because the former are
> all Tommy Atkins, poor fellows, while the continental armies are
> inclusive of the finest brains and temperaments of the land.†

In December 1914 he revealed another concern to his mother:

> Do you know what would hold me together in a battlefield?: The
> sense that I was perpetuating the language in which Keats and the
> rest of them wrote! I do not know in what else England is greatly
> superior, or dearer to me, than another land and people.**

---

* From 'The Ballad of Peace and War', a fragment published in *Wilfred Owen: The complete poems and fragments* edited by Jon Stallworthy, Chatto & Windus, London, 1983, vol. II, p.504.
† *Collected Letters*, p.282.
** Ibid., p.300.

On the one hand he could posture as a patriot, and reveal a love for the English language; on the other, he was detached, self-interested and had an unusually broad vision of Europe as a cultural entity. He had come a long way from Shrewsbury, without yet being able to sort out and reconcile contradictory influences and impressions.

In September 1914 he visited the wounded soldiers in one of the local French hospitals, and learnt some of the realities of war, but still did not think of fighting. Instead he was thinking of all kinds of ways of making money to buy more time for himself in order to become a writer. In a carefully drafted letter of 5 March 1915 he wrote of his ambitions of being a poet and that 'to struggle vulgarly with fist and brick-end, I do refuse.' * However as the summer of 1915 approached, his letters were mentioning the war more and more, and there was a growing determination to get involved and fight. 'I don't want the bore of training, I don't want to wear khaki; nor yet to save my honour before inquisitive grand-children fifty years hence. But I *now do* most *intensely want to fight.*' † And he found comfort in the thought of the distinguished artists who had been members of the Artists' Rifles, which regiment he was now thinking of joining. By October he had finally decided to do so. His war career had started, after a gestation of more than a year.

Joining the army

In his early days of army training, Wilfred Owen frequented the Poetry Bookshop in Devonshire Street, London, where Harold Monro (1879– 1932), its proprietor, also edited *The Poetry Review* and published under the editorship of Edward Marsh (1872–1953) collections of Georgian poetry—anthologies of contemporary poetry of a lyrical and conservative nature. At that time Siegfried Sassoon (1886–1967) and Robert Graves (*b*.1895) whom Owen was to meet and from whom he was to receive great encouragement, counted themselves as Georgians. Monro read some of Owen's sonnets, praising them and advising him on their content. On 4 June 1916, after nine months of training, Owen became a 2nd Lieutenant in the 5th Battalion of the Manchester Regiment. He still found time to read A.E. Housman's (1859–1936) *A Shropshire Lad* and Tennyson's *Tiresias* and worked on a very few poems of his own ('Storm', 'Music' and 'A New Heaven'). Though he had outwardly become an officer, determined that 'if I have got to be a soldier, I must be a good one, anything else is unthinkable,' ** he was now inwardly a poet.

He had grown to become one in relative isolation. His reading had

---

* *Collected Letters*, p.325.
† Letter to Susan Owen, June 1914. Ibid., p.341.
** Harold Owen, *Journey from Obscurity*, Vol. III, p.155.

not been extensive and had been inclined towards the emotive and aesthetic poets of the nineteenth century. Owen remained romantic rather than intellectual; his aestheticism was not the product of an inner conviction but was emotional and derivative. A revealing comparison can be made with his Londoner contemporary, the poet Isaac Rosenberg (1890–1918) who was more closely in touch with other writers, had critics and mentors who guided his reading which was far wider than Owen's, including for example the metaphysical poets as well as philosophers. Owen had no-one in his immediate circle who was well qualified to guide his development as a poet. His most significant literary encounters did not take place until after his twenty-fourth birthday when he met Siegfried Sassoon, and through him other literary figures. Until then he had only his cousin and near contemporary, E. Leslie Gunston, who also wrote poems and with whom he corresponded and in a sense competed in versifying on the most friendly of terms. At a later stage they were joined by a friend, Olwen Joergens. This trio stimulated each other in writing, and though few if any of the poems have stood the test of time, it was by such practice that Owen learnt something of the craft of verse. The recurring theme of loneliness in Owen's poetry, quite apart from its conventional place in romantic poetry, may well have stemmed from his real isolation. 'I am alone among the Unseen Voices',* as he wrote in 1911.

Active service

Owen was drafted to France on the last day of 1916. On 1 January 1917 he was ordered to join the 2nd Manchesters, a regular regiment of experienced soldiers. Within a few days he was in two feet of water in the cold and muddy trenches and fighting in No Man's Land, seeing the men of his company killed and maimed around him. On 30 January he was greatly relieved to receive an order to attend a Course of Instruction in Transport Duties, but in March was back in the trenches. His letters home became more cheerful and less complaining as time passed; certainly they contain none of the pre-army days' self-concerned hypochondria, fostered by his mother. On the night of 13/14 March he fell down a deep hole (maybe a well), hitting the back of his head on the way down. This resulted in concussion and he was in hospital for two weeks, reading the poems of Elizabeth Barrett Browning and writing charming and good-humoured letters home, one containing the 'Sonnet with an Identity Disc' addressed to his youngest brother Colin (the 'sweet friend' of line 12). Discharged from hospital, he went straight

---

* Fragment quoted by Blunden in his edition of the poems, p.7, and by Stallworthy in his complete edition, Vol. 2, p.388.

back to the line of battle, being shelled continually for four days and nights near St Quentin, reconnoitring at night in No Man's Land, and 'going over the top' of the trenches in order to capture a new post. These horrifying experiences gave material for many of his war poems, most of which were not to be written until he was sent back to Britain.

On 1 May, Owen's commanding officer noticed that he was shaky and confused in speech. The concussion and the battle experiences had been too much for him. He was sent to the casualty clearing station and was diagnosed as suffering from 'Neurasthenia', or shell-shock. In a letter to his sister Mary he wrote that it was not the fighting, the Boche (slang for 'Germans'), nor the explosives, but having to shelter for a long time with the scattered remains of one of his comrades.* He also wrote a significant letter home to his mother (?16 May 1917):

> Already I have comprehended a light which never will filter into the dogma of any national church: namely that one of Christ's essential commands was: Passivity at any price! Suffer dishonour and disgrace; but never resort to arms. Be bullied, be outraged, be killed; but do not kill. It may be a chimerical and ignominious principle, but there it is. It can only be ignored: and I think pulpit professionals are ignoring it very skilfully and successfully.... And am I not myself a conscientious objector with a very scared conscience?†

These were the pacifist sentiments that were to infuse his war poems and that were to win him the devotion of left-wing poets and writers of the 1930s, most notably W.H. Auden (1907–73), Stephen Spender (*b*.1909), Cecil Day Lewis (1904–72), and Louis MacNeice (1907–63). His ability to empathise with suffering, and his indignation against the callousness of the war-mongering authorities were readily translated by these writers into political and revolutionary terms. Owen himself, however, kept romantic individuality as his principle, and there is no evidence in his writings that he was concerned with politics of any kind.

Owen was sent back to England in June 1917 when he appeared before a Medical Board. The Board reported that there was little abnormality to be observed but that he was of a 'highly-strung' temperament. He was described as unfit for service for six months and sent to Craiglockhart War Hospital, Edinburgh, for observation and treatment.

Craiglockhart War Hospital, Sassoon and London

His time at Craiglockhart from June until October 1917 was to be of great importance to his development as a poet, chiefly because of his

---

* *Collected Letters*, p.456.
† Ibid., p.461.

encounter with Siegfried Sassoon in August. In the period from June to August he wrote a sonnet, 'The Fates', an unfinished ballad in the style of Sir Walter Scott (1771–1832) and began, more successfully, as a remedial exercise at the suggestion of his doctor, a blank verse epic on the mythological encounter of Hercules and Antaeus. (Antaeus was the giant who derived strength from contact with the earth.) This was never finished. He then became editor of the hospital magazine, *The Hydra*, in which he published for the first time a poem of his own, 'Song of Songs', (1 September 1917), and was kept busy with visitors, visits and therapeutic hospital activities. He acted in a play and probably drafted a play himself, the purpose of which was to 'expose war to the criticism of reason'.* In August, a few weeks after the arrival of Siegfried Sassoon, who was sent to Craiglockhart by the military authorities as an uncontroversial way of silencing his criticisms of the continuing war, Owen plucked up courage to visit him. He had been reading Sassoon's war poems in the collection, *The Old Huntsman* † and had written to his mother:

> I have just been reading Siegfried Sassoon, and am feeling at a very high pitch of emotion. Nothing like his trench life sketches has ever been written or ever will be written.**

Sassoon was to exert a beneficial influence, both on Owen's writing and on his social life. He took a detailed interest in the poems that Owen showed him and advised him to be more direct and more simple in his writing.

> Wasn't it after he got to know me that he first began to risk using colloquialisms which were at that time so frequent in my verses? . . .

> I was sometimes a little severe on what he showed me, censuring the over-luscious writing in his immature pieces, and putting my finger on 'She dreams of golden gardens and sweet glooms' as an example. But it was the emotional element, even more than its verbal expression, which seemed to need refinement. There was an almost embarrassing sweetness in the sentiment of some of his work, though it showed skill in rich and melodious combinations of words. This weakness, as hardly requires pointing out, he was progressively discarding during the last year of his life.‡

Owen wrote 'My Shy Hand', 'Six o'clock in Princes Street', 'The Next

* Quoted in Jon Stallworthy, *Wilfred Owen: A Biography*, Oxford University Press, London, 1974.
† William Heinemann, London, 1917.
** *Collected Letters*, p.484.
‡ Siegfried Sassoon, *Siegfried's journey: 1916–1920*, Faber & Faber, London, 1945, pp.60, 59.

War', and 'Anthem for Doomed Youth', having tried to take Sassoon's advice to heart. On Saturday, 13 October, he met Robert Graves, who had come to visit Sassoon. Owen showed him his draft of 'Disabled' and Graves was 'mightily impressed'. In the following week, encouraged by Sassoon's and Graves's interest Owen wrote or reworked several poems: 'Disabled', 'Dulce Et Decorum Est', 'Winter Song', 'Sonnets to a Child', his sonnet 'Music' and perhaps also 'Greater Love'.

At Craiglockhart Owen experimented in a sustained way with pararhyme (see Part 3, pp.71–3), though there are signs of an interest in it as early as 1912. Owen showed Sassoon his 'Song of Songs' which employed this form of rhyme. Sassoon pronounced the poem 'perfect' and Owen was encouraged to continue these experiments in 'Has Your Soul Sipped?' and 'From My Diary, July 1914'. These three poems are the first fully worked out examples of this remarkable poetic innovation of Owen's. Robert Graves was to write to him in December 1917:

> Don't make any mistake, Owen, you are a damned fine poet already and are going to be more so—I won't have the impertinence to criticize—you have found a new method and must work it yourself—those assonances* instead of rhymes are fine—Did you know that it was a trick of Welsh poetry or was it instinct? †

At the end of October 1917, the Medical Board pronounced Owen fit for service. After a few weeks' leave he was to be sent away to Scarborough. At their parting Sassoon gave him an introduction to Robert Ross (1869–1918), Oscar Wilde's editor and friend, and a London literary pundit. Owen was immensely grateful for Sassoon's friendship and encouragement, and wrote, using imagery from 'O World of many Worlds':

> . . . You have *fixed* my Life—however short. You did not light me: I was always a mad comet; but you have fixed me. I spun round you a satellite for a month, but I shall swing out soon, a dark star in orbit where you will blaze.**

Through Robert Ross, he met the novelists Arnold Bennett (1867–1931) and H.G. Wells (1866–1946), and the poet and novelist Osbert Sitwell (1892–1969). He also met Munro again, and had dealings with the editor of *The Nation*, a magazine critical of the war, where three of his poems were eventually to be published. This short period before his next posting to Scarborough, as Camp Commandant of the Officers' quarters of his Manchester Battalion, was a great success, due entirely

---

* 'assonances': a loosely used term by Graves; more correctly: 'consonances'.
† *Collected Letters*, Appendix C, p.595.
** Ibid., p.505.

to Sassoon's introductions. Owen wrote to his mother on 31 December 1917:

> I am not dissatisfied with my years. Everything has been done in bouts:
>
> Bouts of awful labour at Shrewsbury and Bordeaux; bouts of amazing pleasure in the Pyrenees, and play at Craiglockhart; bouts of religion at Dunsden; bouts of horrible danger on the Somme; bouts of poetry always; of your affection always; of sympathy for the oppressed always.
>
> I go out of this year a Poet, my dear Mother, as which I did not enter it. I am held peer by the Georgians; I am a poet's poet.
>
> I am started. The tugs have left me; I feel the great swelling of the open sea taking my galleon.*

It was natural that Owen should consider himself a Georgian. He had recently read much of what the Georgians had published, and as Sassoon and Graves then allied themselves to the group, he also identified himself with this, the only contemporary English poetic movement with which he was familiar, though he was never to be included in one of Marsh's Georgian anthologies. That he was in any case too passionate a writer to be considered a Georgian by posterity is another matter. Though this New Year's Eve letter contains an ecstatic vision of his own development as a poet, it continues and ends with a vision of the suffering of the soldiers on the battlefield:

> But chiefly I thought of the very strange look on all the faces in that camp; an incomprehensible look, which a man will never see in England . . . It was not despair, or terror, it was more terrible than terror, for it was a blindfold look, and without expression, like a dead rabbit's.
>
> It will never be painted, and no actor will ever seize it. And to describe it, I think I must go back and be with them.†

Owen now saw himself as having a part to play in the war: he was to voice what these soldiers were experiencing, to speak for those who could not speak for themselves.

While stationed at Scarborough, Owen worked on his poem 'The Show', 'Cramped in that funnelled hole', and 'Exposure' all inspired by his reading the French novelist Henri Barbusse's (1873–1935) *Under Fire*, a vivid and horrifying account of the realities of fighting. It is typical of Owen that he had to read about experiences paralleling his own before he could write about what he himself had lived through.

* *Collected Letters*, p.520.
† Ibid., p.521.

He was enjoying his work in Scarborough running the Officers' Mess, and started to plan for his life after the war. He collected some items of furniture for the cottage he dreamt of having.

In January 1918 there was a major mining disaster at Helmerend: a pit explosion killed 155 miners. Owen quickly wrote a poem about it, 'Miners'. To his delight it was accepted by the editor of *The Nation* and a few days later appeared in print. It was his first poem in a national magazine. At the same time he was also invited to Robert Graves's wedding which, unlike Graves himself, he found 'nothing extraordinary'.

March 1918 saw him transferred to Ripon where he found himself a room in a cottage. After his day's work he would write. 'Futility', 'Arms and the Boy', 'Strange Meeting', 'Mental Cases', and 'The Send-Off' are probably all poems from this period. A short leave in May allowed him to visit London where he extended the circle of his literary acquaintances. He met, among others, Charles Scott-Moncrieff (1889–1930) who was to become the translator of Proust and who took an interest in Owen's new pararhyming technique. He wrote excitedly to his mother that his literary reception in London had been magnificent. 'The upshot is that I am to have my work typed at once, and send it to Heinemann, who is certain to send it to Ross to read for him!! This is very subtle. Ross first meant to take it himself but we thought this independent idea a great joke!'* The Sitwells requested in June poems for their 1918 anthology *Wheels*, an annual selection of contemporary poetry edited by Edith Sitwell (1887–1964). Owen was beginning to be aware of the recognition of his peers—his definition of fame.†

The significance of his friendship with Sassoon at Craiglockhart cannot be overemphasised. Sassoon was wealthy, talented and well-connected. It was through him that Owen was given the chance to publish, both by *The Nation* and by the Sitwells. One cannot help wondering what the quality of Owen's poetry and his reputation would have been without Sassoon's encouragement, tactful criticism and introduction to the then rather exclusive circle of the literary élite.

In July Owen started to sort through his poems for Heinemann's, deciding on *Disabled and Other Poems* as its title. His famous Preface (see Part 3, pp.60-1): 'This book is not about heroes . . . ' was probably drafted in his cottage room at Ripon in May 1918 and shows that his war experiences had tempered his adulatory relationship with the Romantic–Victorian poetic tradition as far as its cult of beauty was concerned. He was beginning to seek and find his own voice. But he retained his empathy with the writings of Keats and Shelley, particularly

* *Collected Letters*, p.552.
† Ibid., p.553.

with the latter's reforming fervour. In January 1918 Owen had written to Leslie Gunston: 'Did poetry ever stand still? You can hark back if you will, and be deliberately archaic, but don't make yourself a lagoon, salved from the ebbing tide of the Victorian Age.' His early death, however, put an end to his full development away from the formative influences of the Romantics.

July 1918 saw Sassoon back in London, wounded. Owen visited him and seemed determined after that visit to return to the front himself. With Sassoon away from the battle line, Owen felt that there was no one else to protest against the war and to voice the sufferings of the soldiers. He felt a deep comradeship towards his men, a bond 'wound with war's hard wire' while England seemed full of empty nationalistic propaganda, and war profiteering. To these young soldier poets, England was 'Two Nations': the comfortable and uncomprehending civilians and the needlessly suffering soldiers. Owen felt that his place was with his fighting comrades. Late in August 1918 he was certified fit for service and by the end of the month was again at the base camp at Etaples. His letters before the embarkation record a sadness and a premonition that he would die.

Last months in France

Owen did not engage in fighting at once. He continued with his reading (still Swinburne and Shelley), wrote 'Smile, Smile, Smile' and redrafted several of his Craiglockhart war poems, 'Exposure', 'The Sentry' and 'Spring Offensive'. There is a deep pessimism in all these poems.

During the period 29 September to 3 October 1918 his battalion carried out a successful assault on the Beaurevoir-Fousomme line. Many of his men were killed, but Owen fought bravely and was awarded the Military Cross for his gallantry. This meant a lot to him. It cancelled the imputation that he was unfit to command troops which his neurasthenia of 1917 had carried with it. He wrote to his mother on 4 October:

> I came out in order to help these boys—directly by leading them as well as an officer can; indirectly, by watching their suffering that I may speak of them as well as a pleader can. I have done the first.*

And to Siegfried Sassoon on 10 October:

> I shall feel again as soon as I dare, but now I must not. I don't take the cigarette out of my mouth when I write Deceased over the letters ... I'm glad I've been recommended for M.C. and hope to get it, for the confidence it may give me at home.†

* *Collected Letters*, p.580.
† Ibid., p.581.

On the night of 3/4 November Owen and his men tried to cross the Sambre Canal, advancing on the retreating Germans. It was an almost impossible task. The Germans were well entrenched on the far bank and covered the Manchesters and the Royal Engineers, who were constructing a makeshift bridge, with machine-gun fire. As the men struggled with the bridge and were shot down, Owen was at the water's edge giving encouragement and help. Thus it was that he was hit and killed. With dreadful irony, it was on the day of the Armistice, 11 November 1918, that the news of his death reached his parents.

It is now possible to see that his gifts were not only gifts of genius, but other gifts that only the gods bestow. He came to the war with his imagination in large measure conditioned and prepared to receive and record the experience of the trenches. Botany and Broxton, Uriconium, and Keats, his adolescent hypochondria, his religious upbringing and later doubts, all shaped him for his subject, as for no other. He wrote more eloquently than other poets of the tragedy of boys killed in battle, because he felt that tragedy more acutely, and his later elegies spring from his early preoccupations as flowers from their stem.*

A note on the text

Owen died before he could see more than five of his poems in print.†
Thus from the numerous drafts that exist of many of his poems it is often difficult to decide exactly what his final wording would have been. Apart from a youthful (1913) fantasy of publishing a collection of verse: *Minor Poems—in Minor keys—by a Minor*, and plans for a projected volume at the Casualty Clearing Station (1917) which was to have a purple cover, his serious plans for a published collection date from May 1918. Robert Ross was to assist him in placing it with Heinemann's who had published books by Sassoon and Graves. Though Sassoon had at first been cautious at Craiglockhart and advised Owen against early publication, he changed his mind as he came to know Owen and his work better during that formative summer of 1917. Then he urged him to submit his work to Heinemann, but Owen was slow in acting on this advice.

In July 1918, the Sitwells asked for poems for their annual anthology,

---

* Jon Stallworthy, *Wilfred Owen: A Biography*, Oxford University Press Paperback, Oxford, 1977 and 1983, p.281.
† Poems published in Owen's lifetime: (1) 'Song of Songs' in *The Hydra* (anonymously), 1 September 1917; (2) 'The Next War' in *The Hydra* (anonymously), 29 September 1917; (3) 'Miners' in *The Nation*, 26 January 1918; (4) 'Futility' and 'Hospital Barge at Cérisy', in *The Nation*, 15 June 1918. 'Song of Songs' was also published in *The Bookman*, May 1918, where it had won a consolation prize in a poetry competition.

Wheels, and Owen sent some, but they were only included in the 1919 volume. In 1920 the first edition of Owen's poetry appeared, edited by Sassoon, though Edith Sitwell, it seems, did most of the work. It contained twenty-three poems and was published by Chatto & Windus who since then have been his publishers, or at least involved in his publications. In 1931 the poet and scholar Edmund Blunden (1896–1974) compiled an edition of fifty-nine of the poems together with some notes and a memoir. In 1963 C. Day Lewis edited eighty of the poems, including in his edition more information on the texts and their variants. He drew on the scholarship of D.S.R. Welland, whose *Wilfred Owen: A Critical Study* (1960) was the first monograph on the poet (see Part 5, Suggestions for further reading, p.87).

Dominic Hibberd produced in 1973 an edition of fifty-six of the poems interspersed with extracts from the letters (again published by Chatto & Windus). His notes and introduction are inspired and scholarly, and are a pleasure to read. His suppositions about the dating of certain poems have, however, been superseded by the work of Jon Stallworthy. In 1983 the long-awaited edition of all the poetic writings (177 completed and incomplete poems in all), the variant manuscripts and the fragments (of sixty-seven incomplete poems) was published in two expensive volumes by Chatto & Windus in conjunction with the Hogarth Press and Oxford University Press. The editor is the poet and scholar Jon Stallworthy (*b.*1935) who has compiled the chronology of the poems by a painstaking examination of the paper and handwriting, and comparison with the dated letters. The dating of the poems had hitherto been a problem, and critics until 1983 had had to rely on conflicting internal evidence. Stallworthy's work has made it clear that many of the poems were written over a considerable period, the redrafting in many cases taking more than six months.

Owen's delightful letters (in W.B. Yeats's opinion, Owen was 'a bad poet though a good letter writer'*) have been edited by Harold Owen and John Bell and published by Oxford University Press in 1967. No study of Owen's poetry can be made without reference to his letters; in this as in many other respects he resembles Keats on whom he modelled himself and whose letters he knew well.

Nine of Owen's poems were used by the composer Benjamin Britten (1913–76) in his *War Requiem* (Opus 66, composed 1961), first performed in May 1962 in the New Coventry Cathedral, rebuilt after having been destroyed by bombing during the Second World War. The poems used by Britten were:
(1) 'Anthem for Doomed Youth'

* *Letters on Poetry from W.B. Yeats to Dorothy Wellesley*, Oxford University Press, London, 1940, pp.128–9.

(2) 'Bugles sang, saddening the evening air'
(3) 'The Next War'
(4) 'Sonnet: on seeing a piece of our heavy artillery brought into action'
(5) 'Futility'
(6) 'The Parable of the Old Man and the Young'
(7) 'The End'
(8) 'At a Calvary near the Ancre'
(9) 'Strange Meeting'

Part 2

Summaries

of SELECTED POEMS

THE POEMS DISCUSSED IN THIS SECTION are contained in both C. Day Lewis's and Dominic Hibberd's editions. While others, whether contained in one of these two selections or exclusively in Stallworthy's complete edition, are certainly worthy of commentary, lack of space prevents their inclusion. However, it is hoped that the example set by the critical method employed in this section will enable the student to analyse more of the poems—most notably: 'The Unreturning' (1913 and 1917), 'Music' (1916/17), 'Maundy Thursday' (1917/18), 'Has Your Soul Sipped?' (August 1917), '1914' (autumn 1917), 'The End' (late 1916/17), 'Le Christianisme' (December 1917), 'Cramped in that funnelled hole' (December 1917), 'Hospital Barge at Cérisy' (December 1917), 'Asleep' (1917 and 1918), 'S.I.W.' (1917/spring 1918), 'My Shy Hand' (February 1918), 'Conscious' (early 1918), 'The Send-Off', (May 1918), 'The Calls' (? May 1918), 'A Terre' (July 1918), 'Mental Cases' (1918), 'The Kind Ghosts' (? July 1918), 'The Parable of the Old Man and the Young' (July 1918), 'The Next War' (September 1917/ July 1918), 'Shadwell Stair' (August 1918), and 'Smile, Smile, Smile' (September 1918). Each poem discussed is dated according to Stallworthy's findings, but the order in which they are considered is that of Hibberd's 1973 edition.

On My Songs

This sonnet was drafted at Dunsden on 4 January 1913, influenced by the American poet James Russell Lavell's (1819–1891) sonnet 'To the Spirit of Keats' in which Keats's genius is seen as comforting the struggling and aspiring poet. Owen revised his poem sometime late in 1917. C. Day Lewis gives 'head' in line 8, whereas Hibberd and Stallworthy give 'heart'. Owen wrote many sonnets, most dating from his pre-army days, though two of his most famous war poems are in the sonnet form: 'Sonnet to My Friend: with an identity disc' and 'Anthem for Doomed Youth'. He became a competent practitioner of this form and was able to use it to express a range of emotions: youthful self-revelation, or rhetorical grandeur ('The End' and 'On seeing a Piece of Our Artillery . . . '), or the elegiac lamentation of 'Anthem for Doomed Youth'.

A sonnet is a fourteen-line poem with an elaborate rhyme scheme, usually written in a single stanza, though seldom appearing as such in Owen's poetry. Sometimes he makes a break between the eighth and ninth lines, sometimes he divides the sonnet into four parts with two stanzas of four lines and two stanzas of three lines. Sonnets normally have two main parts: first an octave, that is eight lines, and then a sestet of six lines. In English the metre is usually iambic pentameter as is the case with 'On My Songs'. Sonnets are either based on the Petrarchan form (Francesco Petrarca, 1304–74) or the Shakespearean form (William Shakespeare, 1564–1616)—the two being distinguished by their rhyme schemes which greatly affect the way the subject matter can be stated. The Petrarchan sonnet (rhyme scheme: *abbaabba cdccdc*, or *cdecde*) lends itself to stating a problem or situation in the octave with a resolution in the sestet. The Shakespearean sonnet (rhyme scheme: *ababcdcdefefgg*) allows greater freedom—for example, repetition and variations of the original idea, concluding with an epigrammatic twist.

This particular sonnet of Owen's and most of his others are close to the Shakespearean form, though he wrote Petrarchan sonnets, following the example of Keats (for example, 'Hospital Barge at Cérisy'). C. Day Lewis places 'On My Songs' among the minor poems or juvenilia in the contents list of his collected edition. Nevertheless, it is a key work in the understanding of Owen's life and poetry. He wrote it out in the letter of 4 January 1913 to his mother. This letter would have described in some detail the break he made with religion at the end of his Dunsden stay, but unfortunately it has been irrevocably censored by Harold Owen. However, it records 'I have murdered my false creed' (religion) and speaks of the 'ancient desire of my heart to be like the immortals, the immortals of earthly Fame, I mean'. Rejecting religion was also a way of rejecting, or at least growing away from, his mother to whom religion seemed to matter above all else. It can be no accident that line 10 introduces the image of the motherless child. The poem marks a formative stage in Owen's development away from childhood influences. Thus, too, the 'unseen Poets' are not enough to comfort him, he has to find his own voice.

The break with religion was caused in part by what he considered to be the hypocrisy of the church in the face of the sufferings of the poor. Here there is a parallel to be drawn with his later reactions to the sufferings of the soldiers on the front. Then he was to rebel against the perpetrators of the war and their smug supporters, comfortable at home. There is a further parallel in the ending of the poem: though the lines were created out of a mood of dejection, yet the paradoxical power of poetry might give consolation and comfort to the reader. In the same way the Preface (see Part 3, pp.60–1) to his war poems expresses the hope that what has sprung from even darker moments in his life will one day bring consolation to later generations, though he was unable to end his later war poems on a hopeful note.

The gloom (line 10), night (line 12) and dark (line 13) show an early use of the idea of darkness that was often to recur in later poems. Darkness seemed to be part of the horror of hell and suffering for him, but also it was the proper environment of the lone poet, the 'mad comet', as he saw himself.

The poem shows his tendency to identify with Romantic poets (the 'unseen Poets' of line 1), especially those who died young. But though the poem is derivative and conventionally melancholic, it contains strong feelings struggling to be heard.

NOTES AND GLOSSARY:

rime:	Owen often used this (legitimate but slightly archaic) spelling of 'rhyme'
fraught:	laden, burdened, troubled
shouldst:	archaic form of 'should'
haply:	archaic for 'by chance' or 'perhaps'

O World of many Worlds

This poem was probably begun late in 1912 at Dunsden and revised in France two years later. It again concerns his self-image and his role as an artist, questions which he had to confront as his artistic aspiration began to clash more and more with his duties in the church. It tries to convey a sense of the inevitable, mechanical motion of life and of his struggle to avoid becoming a part of this machinery. The cosmological scale of the poem can be compared with that of 'The Show' (see p.48). In stanza 3, Fate (that is, the role of good fortune in the poet's career) helps him to stand 'where but few advance', as indeed was to happen in 1917 when he met Sassoon. His letter to Sassoon of 5 November 1917 expresses a fulfilment of this poem's view of himself (see Part 1, p.15). Stanza 5 shows concern with the hearts of men which will manifest itself in the empathy of his later war poems, but in stanza 6 he rejects the fixed course of their lives, as happens also in 'Strange Meeting', an image with some roots in the rejection of his mother's fatalistic religion. In stanza 7 he describes himself as a meteor, a romantic image of the artist, who is alone and outside the law and has the task of arousing the imagination of conventional men. The price of this is loneliness— 'Blackness of darkness is my meed for ever?'—which, however, is seen as a glorious state in stanza 9. Poets are givers of light, 'Fair aureoles/ Self-radiated', and when comprehended by ordinary men, that is, when these 'stars' have struck earth, they gather fame, 'many satellites', because they are of more value than the sun itself. The attempted flourish of the poem's ending is almost bathetic. The cosmological metaphor has been taken a little too far; it seems unlikely that poets are more valuable than the sun. Alas, there is hardly an original idea or image in this poem. But it shows Owen dreaming of and schooling himself for fame. It reveals his indebtedness to Keats (*Hyperion*), Shelley *(Adonais,* 'O World, O Life, O Time'), and the Indian poet Rabindranath Tagore (1861–1941) (*Gitamjali*) in its cosmological imagery, and in the development of his romantic individualism which was part of his poetic stance until his death. Stanza 8 is almost a quotation from the Bible (Jude 13): 'Wandering stars, to whom is reserved the blackness of darkness for ever', where the wandering stars are heretics, as Owen was in the eyes of the Vicar of Dunsden at that time. Owen quotes this biblical verse in his letter of 26 April 1913. Though the poem heralds some of his later developments and concerns, it contrasts clearly with his war poems and his later view of the function of poetry. In his Preface of 1918 he states that 'All a poet can do today is warn.' This warning is not of the 'wider ways unknown' of stanza 7, but it *is* to move humanity 'with heavenly fears . . . ' about the realities of war. Owen was then to see himself less as a lawless meteor scorning the destinies of common people and more as a participant in and spokesman for suffering.

NOTES AND GLOSSARY:

meteor:	a shooting star, that is, a lump of rock heated to incandescence by passing from space into the earth's atmosphere
Spanless:	from 'span': literally the utmost distance between tip of thumb and little finger, figuratively any measurable distance
wend:	(*archaic*) go
meed:	(*poetic only*) reward
bourne:	boundary; domain
aureoles:	haloes, circles of light
astern:	near the stern (of a ship); (*figuratively*) behind

From My Diary, July 1914

Despite the title the poem was not drafted until the autumn of 1917, but refers to the summer when Owen was a private tutor in the French Pyrenees, where he arrived on 31 July 1914. Presumably the poem is deliberately dated July, rather than August, to avoid any reference to the outbreak of the war. If, as must be supposed, this poem reflects his memories and preoccupations of that summer, he was very little affected by the news of the outbreak of the war, as his letters indeed indicate. The poem has similarities with 'Song of Songs' (p.31), most notably in its ecstatic incantatory form. The poem, until the work on the chronology was completed by Stallworthy, had been assumed to be a very early example of Owen's pararhyme. We now know that it belongs to the period when Owen generally started to develop this device (his only formal innovation, by the way; see p.63–4 and p.71). As well as the introductory pararhymes 'leaves'/'lives', 'Birds'/'Bards', the longer lines, ending in perfect masculine rhymes, are full of elaborate assonance and alliteration, for example, 'Cheerily chirping in the early day' ('cheer' and 'chir' are pararhymes or consonances while 'chir' rhymes with 'ear'). There has been considerable discussion of Owen's pararhymes, with conflicting nomenclatures. For the best of these discussions and for a suggested standard usage of terminology, the reader should refer to Sven Bäckman's *Tradition Transformed: Studies in the Poetry of Wilfred Owen*, Gleerup, Lund, 1979, pp.168–91. However, the issue need not be complicated.

There are two sorts of full or perfect rhymes: masculine rhyme—a single monosyllabic rhyme, for example, 'cold/gold', and feminine rhyme—when words of two or more syllables rhyme, for example, 'daughters/waters'. Rhymes can be at the end of a verse (a line) of poetry, or they can occur internally, for example, 'In mist or *cloud*, on mast or *shroud*' (from Samuel Taylor Coleridge's (1772–1834) 'The Rhyme of the Ancient Mariner'). The correspondence of rhymed sounds must be exact to be called perfect or full rhyme. When the sounds do not rhyme exactly, they are known as imperfect rhymes, half-rhymes or pararhymes. Generally speaking, pararhymes depend on a repetition of the final consonant sound (sometimes the initial consonants correspond as well) without the correspondence of the vowel sound, for example, 'up/step' or 'Leaves/Lives'. Pararhyming, the term generally reserved for end rhymes, is very little different from consonance, which is the term generally used for the close repetition of identical consonant sounds in a line of verse, for example '*Ch*eer*i*ly *chir*ping'. Alliteration is the term used when only the first consonants in the words are repeated in a line of verse, for example, '*w*ent *w*alking *w*ith *s*low *s*teps . . .' (W.B. Yeats 'The Sad Shepherd'; here the alliteration creates a nice plodding effect). When the same *vowel* sound is repeated in a line of verse without corresponding consonants, the effect is called assonance, for example, 'emb*al*med d*ar*kness' (from Keats's 'Ode to a Nightingale'). These poetic devices can be used merely decoratively, but they can also be used as an integral part of the meaning and mood of a poem. The use of the pararhymes in 'From My Diary, July 1914' is decorative, and the poem cannot be said to achieve anything other than a pleasing description of a summer scene. It is a different matter when the pararhymes of 'Miners' (p.41), 'Insensibility' (p.43), 'Exposure' (p.45), 'The Show' (p.48), and 'Strange Meeting' (p.51) are considered.

This poem, then, represents a significant development in Owen's poetic idiom. Not only is there conscious experimentation with para-rhymes—their conspicuous position and their being balanced by conventional rhymes in each couplet suggest a deliberate parading and yet also a tempering of a new technique, but there is also a freshness in the observations (though nothing unexpected in the choice of subjects) enumerated at random. More than in his earlier juvenilia, the poem is based on direct personal experience and less on his literary models as, for example, in the lines 'Lives/Wakening with wonder in the Pyrenees'. It is difficult not to share in Owen's exuberant enjoyment of his memories of that summer. Nature and love, however, which are the subject matter, are stock themes of the Romantics, and the sensuousness of his descriptions echoes Keats. In fact the last lines are reminiscent of Keats's 'Ode to Psyche' and 'Ode on Melancholy'. Nevertheless, the auditory experimentation shows Owen finding his way towards the virtuoso handling of sound effects in his later war poetry.

NOTES AND GLOSSARY:

myriads:	(*poetic*) vast number
Pyrenees:	a mountain range forming the frontier between France and Spain. Owen worked as a tutor to a family living in the Pyrenees between July and September 1914
Bards:	'bard' means literally a Celtic minstrel and poet. Used poetically to mean any kind of poet
mead:	(*poetic*) meadow, a piece of grassland

Sonnet to My Friend: with an identity disc

The version given in Blunden's, C. Day Lewis's and Hibberd's editions varies considerably from that which Stallworthy gives as the final draft. The poem was first written in March 1917 and revised at Craiglockhart with Sassoon's help later the same year. The differences appear in lines 4–8 and lines 11 and 14 of Stallworthy's version given below:

lines 4–8   I better that; and recollect with shame
             How once I longed to it from life's heats
             Under these holy cypresses, the same
             That keep in shade the quiet place of Keats.

line 11:   But let my death be memoried in this disc.

line 14:   Until the name grow vague and wear away.

Sassoon was responsible for the version of lines 11 and 14 given in the editions by Blunden and others. (They were based on his pencilled amendments made at Craiglockhart.) In all instances, Owen's own final versions seem superior: the sense is clearer, the language more concrete. Shakespeare's Sonnet 104, 'To me, fair friend, you never can be old', was written out by Owen on the back of one of the drafts, but his sonnet owes more to Keats's, 'When I have fears that I may cease to be'. Both Keats's and Owen's sonnets are about the dwindling of previously cherished hopes when the poet is confronted with almost certain death. Both poems are addressed to a beloved friend—Owen's to his youngest brother Colin, to whom an earlier draft was sent in a letter. Owen is saying in the sonnet: I can now better my dream of fame (of having a memorial in Poets' Corner in Westminster Abbey), and I remember with shame my desire to die young and be buried next to Keats in Italy. Now, because war has interrupted my life and work as a poet, there will be no memorial to me, only my identity disc, which, when it is sent home at my death, you, little brother, should wear. Far from having inscriptions made in my memory, let my name on it be worn away by lying next to your heart.

Its sentiment is typical of Owen's 1917–18 poems. The emphasis is on spontaneous expressions of affection, ritualistic behaviour is disparaged and there is a sensuous directness in his depiction of the close human relationship.

NOTES AND GLOSSARY:

identity disc: each British soldier was issued with three little discs bearing his name and number to be worn on a cord round his neck. If he was killed, one of the discs was sent to his next of kin

High in the heart of London: it is clear from the manuscript drafts that Owen was referring to Westminster where there is a Poet's Corner in the Abbey

holy cypresses: Keats died in Italy and was buried among cypress trees in the Protestant Cemetery in Rome

Greater Love

Another poem from his great creative period at Craiglockhart and Ripon (autumn/winter 1917), it was finally revised at Scarborough in July 1918. One of the draft's subtitles is 'To any Woman'. The biblical allusion of the title comes from the Gospel of St John 15: 13, 'Greater love hath no man than this, that a man lay down his life for his friends.' It was included under 'doubtful' in Owen's draft Table of Contents for his projected collection of war poems, which should be borne in mind when assessing it as a statement about the war; it may not represent his final view. Apart from its biblical references, it parodies Swinburne's 'Behind the Mirror'

White rose in the red rose-garden
Is not so white;
Snowdrops that plead for pardon
And pine for fright
Because the hard East blows
Over their maiden vows
Grow not as this face grows from pale to bright.

Such parodies are used in Owen's war poems in order to expose the horror and indignity of war by deliberately contrasting these qualities with familiar attitudes or emotions, for example, romantic love, and by attempting to contain such a contrast in traditional poetic forms. The familiar attitudes and forms are thereby revealed as wholly inadequate at coping with war's realities which the reader is then shocked into recognising.

The poem progresses in a series of images in which ironic and terrible comparisons are made. Red lips (so stock an image that it was already parodied by Shakespeare) mean less than the spilt blood; the love between man and woman seems 'shame' to the pure love of the dying soldier. Even the sexual act is compared with the bayoneted soldier writhing in the agony of death. The voice of the universal woman addressed in the poem pleases less than the memory of the soldiers' voices; the soldiers are capable of greater love; they suffer under her inflicted burden and she is only fit to weep at their sufferings. The insistent negation of the poem is achieved by the syntactic and metrical prominence given to the negative, particularly in its archaic form, 'Trembles not', 'sings not'. In each stanza romantic denial of the first two lines is thrust forward by the rhyme scheme (aa, bbb, a) to the appalling images of the last line. The whole is given declamatory weight by the almost exclusive use of monosyllables—as if Owen were pronouncing a law and a judgement upon beautiful women. There can be no doubt that the poem shows a mastery of form.

'Greater Love' is a poem of personal response to the war rather than one of his other main approach: that of celebrating the comradeship and bravery of his soldiers. It combines three of his major themes in its elaborate and striking parody: sexual love, the soldier in battle and Christ. In the literal meaning of the poem ordinary sexual love is rejected in the face of the suffering soldier, as are conventional poetic attitudes in the Swinburne parody. Yet Owen still keeps the heightened language of Romantic/Victorian poets: 'piteous mouths', 'hearts made great with shot'. The soldier is identified with Christ in stanza 4—he carries the cross or burden of suffering for the sake of others as Christ did. Yet when he suffers, 'God seems not to care', as on Calvary.

Together with this poem's tentative redefinition of God's involvement with humanity there is a misogamy which recurs in many of his poems. Indeed there are few positive references to women in Owen's poetry. The drafts reveal that the love poems, as often as not, are addressed to men or young boys. Not only are the woman's attractions in 'Greater Love' seen as little in comparison to his fighting comrades, but she is also seen as the perpetrator of the war. The cross is one which she inflicts: 'Paler are all which trail/Your cross through flame and hail'. She may however, be allowed to mourn from afar once her sins have been forgiven, as Mary Magdalen was in the garden of the sepulchre. 'Weep, you may weep, for you may touch them not.' (Compare St John 20: 17.) The implication of the poem seems to be that Owen has undergone some great transcendent experience on the battlefield which has nullified ordinary existence and normal sexual relationships and which makes him seek, if not yet find, a new poetic idiom.

NOTES AND GLOSSARY:

eyes blinded: Owen had witnessed the blinding of one of his sentries by a bomb in January 1917. After that there are many references to eyes in his poems

Six o'clock in Princes Street

Again part of the prodigious Craiglockhart output, this poem was written in the late summer/early autumn of 1917. Owen wrote to his mother on 8 August 1917:

At present I am a sick man in hospital, by night; a poet, for quarter of an hour after breakfast; I am whatever and whoever I see while going down to Edinburgh on the train: greengrocer, policeman, shopping lady, errand boy, paper-boy, blind man, crippled Tommy, bank-clerk, carter, all of these in half an hour ... *

He was echoing Keats's 'negative capability', the essential poetic quality of 'filling some other Body' † and of identifying fully with the object of perception, 'if a sparrow come before my Window I take part in its existence and pick about the Gravel'.** The poem is an attempt at putting this Keatsian empathy into practice: 'Or *be* you in the gutter where you stand' (italics mine).

The poet is watching the crowds walking home at the end of the day in Edinburgh's main shopping street, which runs east-west through the

---

* *Collected Letters*, p.480.
† Letter to Richard Woodhouse, 27 October 1818, *Letters of John Keats*, ed. Robert Gittings, Oxford University Press, London, 1970, p.157.
** Op. cit., p.38, letter to Benjamin Bailey, 22 November 1817.

city. There is a wistful envy in 'they have not far to roam . . . gay of eyes' and his own isolation is emphasised: 'In twos and threes, they . . . roam.' The second and third stanzas focus on the boy selling newspapers at the side of the pavement. If only he could be with him, or if he actually became the newspaper boy, holding and dispensing the news of the war, himself a symbol of humanity in the war-torn world, he would be able to abandon his old comforting creeds of orthodox Christianity, 'gleams untrue', and poetic aestheticism, 'tiring after beauty through star-crowds'. This poem has been triggered off by his envy of the shoppers' peace of mind with which he cannot, however, identify because of his knowledge of the suffering brought by the war. Yet he might gain new purpose and a measure of peace if he could proclaim the news of the war or truth about it. Only a month or two before writing this poem, Owen had written the sonnet 'The Fates' which declares a belief in beauty both as an ideal and as an escape from the 'vice and rack of age'. The mood of this sonnet is antithetical to that of 'Six o'clock in Princes Street', and it is significant that the search for a new voice and a new subject is qualified by the conditional 'Dared' of stanza 2 in the later poem. Owen does of course 'dare' to proclaim the horrors of war and does in a sense become the newspaper boy, but his old creeds as revealed in 'The Fates' have never been quite abandoned.

NOTES AND GLOSSARY:

tiring after beauty through star-crowds: the imagery here is reminiscent of 'O World of many Worlds' (p.24), but there may also be an echo from Yeats's 'When you are old' in this line as well as in the last line, 'And all their sorrows in your face'

rain-flawed: critics have commented on the fondness Owen had for elemental imagery and on his successful use of it

---

Song of Songs

Written at Craiglockhart in the summer of 1917, this poem was shown to Siegfried Sassoon who 'pronounced [it] perfect work, absolutely charming, etc. etc. and begged that I would copy it out for him, to show the powers that be.'* It became the first poem of Owen's to be published, albeit in the hospital magazine *The Hydra* (1 September 1917). Later, in May 1918, it received a prize in a poetry competition run by *The Bookman* and was again published.

The poem is of greater interest technically and historically than thematically. To deal with the thematic aspect first, it is rather derivative,

---

* *Collected Letters*, p.486.

reflecting synaesthetic* images and excessively sweet cadences from the Pre-Raphaelites (Christina Rossetti's (1830–94) 'The Echo'), and from Swinburne, Wilde, and so on. (Compare Sassoon's comment, p.14.) It seems more concerned with elaborations of technique and imagery than with real passion. However, it has a stylistic finesse and musical charm in its elaborate euphony which excited Sassoon and helped to win his literary support. Various utterances of the beloved appropriate to the time of day are described in terms of music of a transcendent kind 'the sense that no songs say' (compare 'The End'). Each stanza deals with a part of the day, and is given an ecstatic invocatory quality by the anaphora, or repetition, of the beginning of the first line of each. As well as the pararhyming of each line (laugh/leaf/Life), there are one or more examples of internal assonance, alliteration, consonance and onomatopoeia in each line. It is one of the dozen or so pararhymed poems, of which only this one and 'The Roads Also' are not about war. It is of interest also in that it shows that pararhyming does not necessarily have a dissonant or melancholic effect. Cecil Day Lewis sums up the use of pararhymes when he states that they can 'impart a subdued, sustained melodic tone to verse, and enable the writer to use rhyme words which have grown stale as end-rhymes'.†

NOTES AND GLOSSARY:
viols: medieval stringed instruments from which the violin family of instruments was developed
solaceth: comforts (*archaic ending*)

The Dead-Beat

This poem was written at Craiglockhart in August 1917 after Owen's second encounter with Sassoon in whose style it was deliberately executed. This was his first 'risk [at] using colloquialisms' (see p.14) and of implementing Sassoon's advice on discarding 'the over-luscious writing' and the 'almost embarrassing sweetness in the sentiment of some of his work'. It certainly is a startling contrast with 'Song of Songs' and marks Owen's discovery through Sassoon that his own experiences in the war could be used as a poetic subject. It is a significant development away from the Romantic idea of beauty as the true inspiration and source of poetry. From now on Owen's great war poetry was to be produced. In Owen's draft Table of Contents for his projected collection *Disabled and Other Poems* which he was going to send to Heinemann (see p.17), 'The Dead-Beat' is listed under the

---

* Synaesthetic: merging different kinds of sensory experiences, for instance colour and music.
† In *A Hope for Poetry*, Basil Blackwell, Oxford, 1934, p.74.

heading 'Indifference at Home'. It concerns a private soldier who has completely collapsed in a state of shock and is unable to respond to orders and the commanding officer's threat of shooting him for deserting his post. He cries with pathetic false heroism that he will murder his enemies: 'I'll do 'em in.' One of his comrades explains that he may be more worried about what is going on at home than disturbed by the carnage of the war. He is thinking of the 'valiant' armchair soldiers, the relatives who have pressed him to join up, and of his wife who is being unfaithful to him. It may be her lovers that he wishes to kill. He is sent to a casualty clearing station, though he is unwounded and physically fit. The stretcher-bearers assume that he is malingering, and the Doctor is entirely unsympathetic, so much so that he rejoices when soon after the soldier dies. It is a moral anecdote in rhyme where the breakdown of the soldier (realistically presented as the unattractive condition it is: 'sullenly', 'stupid', 'whines' . . .) is contrasted with the comfort and self-indulgence of the non-combatants at home in Britain. The stretcher-bearers and the doctor too are non-combatants, and the latter is self-indulgent in his drinking habits. The events and contrasting attitudes in the poem (suffering, nervous collapse; self-indulgence, superficial judgements) are calculated to shock the reader into a recognition of the plight of the ordinary soldier and of the need to discard all common notions of cowardice.

NOTES AND GLOSSARY:

Dead-Beat:	(*slang*) beat: exhausted; dead-beat: so exhausted as to feel totally incapacitated. In the poem, the soldier is literally exhausted to death by the war
Blighty:	(*military slang*) Britain
pluck:	(*slang*) courage, literally the plucked guts from game
stiffs:	(*slang*) corpses
Hun:	(*slang*) German
strafe:	(*military slang*) bombardment

Anthem for Doomed Youth

This is one of Owen's most famous poems, and one over which he took great pains. There are several drafts in existence. It was written at Craiglockhart in September-October 1917, and Sassoon suggested amendments and supplied the word 'Anthem' for the title which heralds the poem's solemnity, as the word 'doomed' addresses the millions dead and yet to die. It is written in sonnet form. In the draft Table of Contents for Owen's projected collection of poems for Heinemann, it is listed under the heading of 'Grief', and it is indeed an elegiac lamentation for the young men slaughtered 'as cattle' in the war.

Like many other of Owen's war poems, it works through a series of
contrasts, and here the contrasts are framed as questions followed by
answers. What burial ceremonies are appropriate for those who die in
the war? The answer in the octet is that the sounds of battle are the
appropriate forms of mourning, they function as a wordless lament.
The monstrosity of war seems to negate Christian ritual—the pattered
'hasty orisons' of church prayers are a greater mockery of the sacrifice
the soldiers make than the sounds of the guns. Thus each musical part
of a funeral or memorial service is replaced, booming guns for bells,
repeated rifle shots for mechanically uttered prayers, wailing shells for
choirs. But there is a lamentation in the fact that they are buried far
from home, it is 'only the monstrous anger of the guns . . . ' that accom-
panies their death. The octet ends with a poignant Housmanesque
bugle call from home, the 'sad shires' (perhaps also a reference to the
names of the various regiments), leading into the concluding sestet
which deals not with sounds of mourning on the battlefield, but with
images of mourning at home for the dead who have been denied a funeral ceremony in the presence of their families. Earlier critics tended to
over-emphasise the negation of traditional ceremony in this poem and
Owen's impatience with formal religion, which is certainly one of its
themes, but the whole poem also stands as a lament for the soldiers'
lonely deaths, and for the fact that they are denied proper burial. There
is a dreadful irony in the images of guns, rifles and shells mourning the
men whom they kill and the poem is not without bitterness in the octet
which acts *in toto* as a lament (by the sound association of the imagery
as much as by the sound of the language itself) against the monstrous
form of the soldiers' deaths. The images of the sestet, however, are of
the silent suffering of their families and the soundlessness of these last
six lines brings a form of peace. Tears glimmering in the mourners'
eyes will be as candles held in church by acolytes, the pale faces of the
men's sweethearts will be their funeral cloths, and their graveside
flowers the tender thoughts of those who have patiently waited for
their return from the war. Some of the diction of the sestet, especially
line 12, is over-precious and detracts from the sincerity of the mourning. However, the wonderful image of the last line, though a little
obscure, seems to measure out time in waiting and mourning. The
poem has moved from lament and bitterness in the octet to a celebra-
tion or an honouring of grief in the sestet. Its strength lies in those
images which are aptly and justly chosen to suggest the horror of war,
the inadequacy of religion and the validity of love and grief. It has a
greater compassion and respect for human relationships than Owen's
more acrid poem 'Greater Love' and marks his rapid growth as a poet
in the second half of 1917, inspired by his war experiences, his stay at
Craiglockhart and his encounter with Sassoon.

NOTES AND GLOSSARY:

Anthem: usually extract from the Bible or liturgy, set to sacred music

passing bell: a bell tolled immediately after a death

patter: rapid talk, from *paternoster*, the Lord's Prayer, often said quickly and thoughtlessly because of its familiarity. (Owen occasionally allows himself a pun, for instance, 'salient' in 'Exposure'.) It is also used onomatopoeically to suggest the sound of rapid gunfire

orisons: prayers

shires: counties (formerly territorial divisions of the United Kingdom, each forming an administrative unit). Most regiments bear county names, for example, The Gloucestershire Infantry

pall: cloth used to cover a coffin

Disabled

This is the poem that impressed Robert Graves when he visited Siegfried Sassoon, and met Owen, at Craiglockhart in October 1917. It was drafted then and revised at Scarborough in July 1918.

There are enough verbal echoes of Housman's poem 'To an Athlete Dying Young' in 'Disabled' to make it seem a castigation of Housman's patriotic enthusiasm for war, and indeed all patriotic poetry that made light of disablement and glorified death, for example:

> What if the best of our wages be
> An empty sleeve, a stiff-set knee,
> A crutch for the rest of life—who cares,
> So long as the One Flag floats and dares?*

Owen focuses on the fate of one man, a single victim of war. He is very young, not more than eighteen perhaps, and had joined up for all the wrong reasons, though they were reasons encouraged by official recruiting propaganda, dealt with in stanza 4 (smart uniforms, *esprit de corps*, pay, and so on). Hibberd has pointed out † that the last line of the poem may well echo the recruiting poster slogan of 1914, 'Will they never come?', and the football imagery may reflect recruiting drives made at matches earlier in the war. The first stanza of the poem describes the disabled victim in his dejected state and the radical change in his view of life: cheerful voices of the boys playing in

* W.E. Henly, 'A New Song to an Old Tune', *Poems*, vol. II, London, 1908, p.150.
† 'Some Contemporary Allusions in Poems by Rosenberg, Owen and Sassoon', *Notes and Queries*, August 1979, p.333.

the evening seem 'saddening like a hymn', and their play seen against his disablement creates a composite picture of despair. The second stanza shifts to a year before when he was able to enjoy himself on a night out in Town with girls who now have no interest in him. There is impressionistic magic in the line 'When glow-lamps budded in the light blue trees'—the past has become enchanted and the reality of the present is brought most forcefully to the reader's notice in the line '... before he threw away his knees'. Stanza 3 emphasises his former beauty and his extreme youth, indicting the recruiting officers of stanza 4, and translates his youth into the image of his life-blood which he has poured away into the ground of the battlefield. Stanza 4 remembers with irony his pride at bleeding at football matches. The images of being cheered and carried shoulder-high is a direct reference to Housman's poem. Owen also introduces his recurring theme of the women at home encouraging the war by appealing to men's sexual pride (compare 'Le Christianisme', 'Greater Love', 'The Send-Off'). All three references to women in this poem are pejorative: they are attracted by superficialities, fickle and heartless. The cheering the soldier receives in stanza 5 is not the hero's welcome, it is, obliquely, a priest preparing him for death. And until then, he will live a living death, neglected in an institution. As many of Owen's poetic expositions of war it centres on contrasts. The main contrast is the comparison between the young man's former glory, 'carried shoulder-high', for no better reason than his health and youth, and his present neglect after his huge sacrifice. 'To-night he noticed how the women's eyes/Passed from him to the strong men that were whole.' Unlike some of Owen's earlier anti-war poems, 'Disabled' offers a balance of irony and compassion. He has articulated the suffering of individuals and the loss of any purpose in their lives—the consequences for millions of victims of the war—rather than dealt directly with war itself. This was a growing tendency in his approach to war as a poetic subject. In this poem, women are accused of indifference to suffering: the planners of the war are blamed only implicitly.

More compassionate towards the individual, Owen's later poems employ a plainer diction; there are fewer adjectives in 'Disabled' than in earlier poems, and he allows himself freedom in stanza length and in metric length of line. Actuality of speech now sometimes takes precedence over traditional poetical form (for example, lines 10 and 40), so much so that Graves, whose views on verse form were more conservative, commented on it critically in a letter to Owen.*

NOTES AND GLOSSARY:

mothered: that is, the boys eventually go home to their mothers and to bed

* Letter of *c*. 17 October 1917, *Collected Letters*, Appendix C, p.595.

a peg:	(*slang*) a drink, usually brandy and soda
kilt:	skirt worn by men in Scotland and part of army uniform in Scottish regiments
plaid socks:	thick, hand-knitted, patterned woollen socks worn with kilts and having a dagger inserted in them as part of full (Scottish) Highland dress
Esprit de corps:	(*French*) team or regimental spirit
dole:	give out

Dulce Et Decorum Est

Another Craiglockhart poem from October 1917, revised sometime in early 1918. In Owen's Table of Contents it is under the heading 'Indifference at home'. He sent it to his mother with the words: 'Here is a gas poem, done yesterday . . . The famous Latin tag* means of course *It is sweet and meet to die for one's country. Sweet!* and *decorous!*' .† One of the drafts of this poem bears the dedication 'To Jessie Pope etc'. She and those like her are therefore the 'friend' of line 25. She was a writer of light verse who turned to patriotic themes when the war broke out, and published many verses in the *Daily Mail* and the *Daily Express*, exhorting young men to join up. Owen was greatly concerned about the patriotism of people who knew nothing of the horrors of fighting and 'Dulce Et Decorum Est' is an attempt to outface authors with such views. Here we have the 'maturer' Owen, as it is a poem dictated by truth and not by beauty and one that is part of his movement away from vagueness to greater realism. Its tone, however, is not of compassion but of indignation and bitterness which is at its best both lofty and cutting.

The poem is in four stanzas and four corresponding sections. The first deals with the extreme condition of the exhausted soldiers and is couched in somewhat hyperbolic terms—'All went lame; all blind'—indicating the fervour of Owen's feelings rather than the misery of the men. The images conjured up in this stanza, however, create a devastating contrast with the classically rooted idea of the glory of dying heroically for one's country. The second stanza deals with a gas attack and the cruel death of a soldier, literally drowning in his own blood, unable to put on his protecting mask in time. The isolation of the third stanza of only two lines emphasises the personal reaction of the poet to these circumstances—it seems to indicate a recurring nightmare from his neurasthenia. There is a nightmarish guilt in his inability to help the soldier, 'before my helpless sight', emphasised by the accusatory

* From Horace (65–8BC), *Odes*, III.ii.13.
† *Collected Letters*, pp.499–500.

accusatory: 'He plunges at me.' The fourth stanza addresses the poetess, asking her to consider the scene and then 'The Old Lie: Dulce et decorum est/Pro patria mori'. Again Owen is enlightening through contrast.

As is always the case with Owen, there are some unusually well-chosen words that deepen the poem's meaning and make it vivid: 'haunting flares' which transforms the whole setting of the poem into a nightmare; 'outstripped Five-Nines' literally the bombs are tired, but it is the (transferred) fatigue of the men that makes them seem so; 'ecstasy of fumbling' a phrase which evokes both the sharpness of fear and the clumsiness of exhaustion; the strong image of drowning through the pane of sea-green glass in the mask; 'guttering' which conveys the sounds of the last flickers of life in the moments before a painful death; 'such high zest' which neatly sums up the tone of Jessie Pope's exhortative verses. However, equally typically and in almost equal measure, there are exaggerated or misplaced images and epithets: the heaping of images in lines 1 and 2, 6 and 7—'hags' *and* 'beggars', all lame, blind, deaf *and* drunk; 'a devil's sick of sin'—why would a devil vomit, that is, reject what he stands for and is this really a telling image of the dying man's face?; 'bitter as the cud of vile, incurable sores'—is cud a suitable image of bitterness? Presumably cud is not bitter, since cows chew and regurgitate it several times quite happily. But even when Owen misuses words, he does so with an intensity that is arresting; his misjudgements are balanced by fervour, and it may well be this latter quality that has made the poem one of the best-known of the First World War.

NOTES AND GLOSSARY:

Five-Nines:	5.9 calibre shells
Gas:	phosgene or mustard-gas which burnt the tissues of the lungs, causing internal bleeding
helmet:	mask with glass pane worn for protection against gas
lime:	a caustic substance, that is, a substance which can burn live tissue
guttering:	(1) channel for carrying rain water; (2) when used of candles, melting away by becoming channelled. Used in the poem suggestively; Owen probably meant flickering out like a candle, or gurgling like a draining gutter, referring to the sounds in the throat of the choking man

Inspection

Listed under the heading 'Inhumanity of war' in Owen's Contents, this poem was written and completed at Craiglockhart, August–September

1917, under the influence of Sassoon's war poetry. In its matter-of-factness, it illustrates Owen's declaration (in his Preface) that he was 'not concerned with poetry'. It certainly displays his ear for conversation and his ability to handle colloquial verse.

The poem is in the form of a dramatic dialogue between an officer (the poet himself) and a soldier who has a stain on his uniform on parade. The soldier is punished and when later he tells the officer that the stain was blood, he is told that 'Blood's dirt'. The soldier replies with incisive and ironic religious and military allusions that he and his like are being sacrificed in order to expiate, or make amends for, the guilt of the world and when dead and white (and therefore seemingly clean) they will be ready for the final inspection by God.

The poem opens with the arresting accusation of the officer which contrasts with the hesitant (there is a comma after each word) reply of the soldier. The hypocrisy of the situation becomes apparent with the alluson to Shakespeare's *Macbeth*, the 'damned spot' of Lady Macbeth's guilt (Act V, Scene 1). The soldiers are sent to fight and die, but their blood, or the reality of war, is unsightly and must not be visible, even their youthful red cheeks must be bled white. Here again Owen is castigating ritual, this time army ritual which is translated into religious ritual, that is, sacrifice. And the sacrifice of the soldiers on behalf of warring nations is as hypocritical as trying to wash away the outward signs of sin—like white-washing an army barrack before a Field-Marshal's inspection—for the sin, the world's aggression, still remains. (Compare 'The Parable of the Old Man and the Young'.) The image of the Last Judgement as a military parade is bitter indeed. Will God dispense the same kind of justice as the officer? One is led to presume so, since the war and the sacrifice of the innocent have been allowed to happen. Except for the few last great poems when Owen views war from a distance, or when by avoidance of specific incidents he translates his writing to a plan of universal significance, he does not refer to a common human responsibility for the war. The soldiers are all innocent, victims in the hands of war-mongers, of a callous god and indeed of women also. This belief in innocence is the root of the fierce compassion in his war poetry and must owe a lot to his mother's religious and sexual puritanism. It is at the same time the strength and the weakness of his poetry—it gives intensity while limiting it. And it is easy to see how his compassion for victims could be translated into Marxist terms, as it was by the politically conscious poets and critics of the 1930s.

The poem is the product of an internal quarrel with himself, for he is both the officer who carried out his duties on behalf of the perpetrators of war, and the poet who exposes the situation. Thus there is a duality in the image of the blood—it is a symbol both of guilt and of life, and is used as such or in either way in many of his poems. (Compare 'Mental

Cases', 'Asleep', 'Spring Offensive' and 'The Kind Ghosts'.) Yeats made the perceptive distinction (which he did not think of applying when considering Owen's poetry): 'We make out of the quarrel with others rhetoric but out of the quarrel with ourselves poetry.'* Owen's writing is rhetorical when he quarrels with the older generation in 'The Parable of the Old Man and the Young', with Jessie Pope in 'Dulce Et Decorum Est' and with the Church in 'At a Calvary near the Ancre', but in 'Inspection' he avoids the direct denouncement, the over-emphasis on horror and suffering, and in its colloquialism, culminating in witty and illuminating irony, he lets the reader's imagination play its part in evoking the poet's vision.

Apologia Pro Poemate Meo

Though written in November–December 1917 at Scarborough, this poem seems to be a response to a comment in Robert Graves's letter of late December 1917: 'For God's sake cheer up and write more optimistically—The war's not ended yet but a poet should have a spirit above wars!'† But it is quite likely that Graves had already said as much to Owen earlier. It seems, however, more certain that it is a response to Graves's poem 'Two Fusiliers' which celebrates his and Sassoon's friendship on the battlefield and finds 'Beauty in Death/In dead men breath'. Owen, as if anxious to share in their friendship, responds: 'I, too, saw God through mud.' In so doing he sets up with an internal half-rhyme (God/mud) the fundamental paradox on which the poem is based. The poem, while exposing the horrors of war, celebrates the divine aspect of man which transcends the horrors of battle. In so doing he creates a profounder poem than Graves's homage to his war-time friend.

Owen was faced with the problem of articulating what must be considered the ineffable. His 'Apologia', originally entitled 'The Unsaid', says as much: 'except you share/With them in hell . . . You shall not hear.' More than once he quoted a saying from Rabindranath Tagore in relation to his war experiences: 'When I go from hence let this be my parting word, that what I have seen is unsurpassable.' In order to make his 'unsurpassable' experiences understood he used in his 'Apologia' familiar Romantic-Victorian poetic traditions and honorific terms, such as love, joy, beauty, music, peace, as ironic parallels to life in the trenches. That, paradoxically, such emotions and sensations should emerge from war's horrors gives the reader a shock apposite to the conditions of war, 'the sorrowful dark of hell', while giving these terms a

---

* 'Anima Hominis' (1917), published in *W.B. Yeats: Selected Criticism*, ed. A. Norman Jeffares, Macmillan, London, 1964, and Pan Books, London, 1976.
† *Collected Letters*, Appendix C, p.596.

new meaning in that terrible context. Thus there is merriment amid slaughter (stanzas 1 and 2), exhilaration in transcending fear (stanza 3), and a transformation of ordinary men through self-sacrifice into angels, 'Seraphic for an hour; though they were foul'. Love, as known 'in old song', is surpassed by the fellowship of the soldiers bound by the accoutrements of war: barbed wire, stakes, bandages and rifle-thongs. In these two stanzas (5 and 6), the soft assonances and alliterations of Romantic love—'soft silk of eyes that look and long'—contrast with the hard consonances of pararhymes—'war's hard wire whose stakes are strong;/Bound with the bandage of the arm that drips'. There is beauty in the soldiers' curses; music, that is, emotions that transcend words, in the silence of their work and a paradoxical peace when the bombing is at its most intense.

This is a poem of personal response to the war which relies once again on contrast and paradox in order to convey its meaning. These two qualities are almost intrinsic to First World War poetry when the mechanised warfare and its mass slaughter were so new and shocking that the poetical idiom had to have root in something known or familiar in order to be understood at all, and even so Owen was uncertain that he would be understood, as the last two stanzas reveal.

NOTES AND GLOSSARY:

barrage: gunfire so directed as to make an area impassable

platoon: a small body of soldiers; a battalion is subdivided into companies and companies into platoons

oblation: an offering or sacrifice to a god

seraphic: belonging to the highest order of angels

love is not the binding of fair lips: a reference to Leslie Gunston's poem 'L'amour' in his collection *Sonatas in Silence*, where love is described as 'The binding of lips, the binding of eyes'. Gunston's poems seemed, in the light of the war, out of date to Owen

spate: sudden flood

Miners

While Owen was at Scarborough there was an explosion in a coal mine at Halmerend on 12 January 1918, which killed about one hundred and fifty miners, both men and boys. Owen wrote this poem immediately after reading the newspaper accounts on 13 or 14 January. He claimed in a postcard to Leslie Gunston that he had written it in half an hour. He sent it to *The Nation*, a periodical which had begun to attack the continuation of the war, and it was published there on 26 January. Apart from his poems printed in the Craiglockhart hospital magazine,

The Hydra, this was Owen's first poem to appear in print (see p.19). Owen's own comment on the poem to his mother, quoted by Edmund Blunden* was: 'Wrote a poem on the Colliery Disaster: but I get mixed up with the War at the end. It is short, but oh! sour.'

The poem is in three parts. The first three stanzas set the scene: the poet sits in front of his fire and at first the coal puts him in mind of pre-historic times. Images of fern forests inhabited by animals now extinct, the 'low, sly lives' before birds or men evolved, are conjured up. In the second part of the poem, stanzas 4 and 5, he begins instead to think of the miners killed and dying, 'Writhing for air'. And the white cinders of his fire make him think of white bones (or fossils) of all the dead long gone, killed in other disasters, who have now been forgotten. In stanza 6 he turns to the victims of the war, for death and the 'dark pits' remind him of the trenches. The soldiers' work, digging and fighting for peace is as dangerous and thankless as the miners'. The third part of the poem, stanzas 7 and 8, point to the comfortable future genera-tions, who will be 'well-cheered/By our lives' ember', without thinking of the suffering and death of the soldiers.

The coal in the poet's fire is a symbol of the distant past, of the miners, and by a clever modulation, of the soldiers killed in war. The wistful luxury of the images of the first three stanzas is reminiscent of the natural opulence of 'From my Diary, July 1914' which also uses pararhyme, but 'Miners', typically for Owen's 'maturer' war poetry, contrasts these images with the 'sourness' of the war dead. The new strength depending on this contrast is given emotional intensity by the poet's own identification with the soldiers in the last stanza. The move-ment from the present to the remote past, to the present again and to the war, is achieved by the unifying symbol of the burning coal and the dark tunnels of death and destruction. Fittingly the ending returns above ground to the comfortable firesides of the future generations. Here is an example of symbols and imagery used as integral parts of the poem and not merely decoratively as in 'From my Diary'. Edmund Blunden's remark that Owen, 'is, at moments, an English Verlaine'† seems justified.

The poem is pararhymed throughout, and some pairs of these rhymes descend in pitch (as elsewhere in Owen's poems): simmer/sum-mer, mine/men, lids/lads, and so on, and echo the prominent low-pitched vowels of the latter stanzas: amber, groaned, ground, and so on. This makes the gloom of the poem more intense. The onomatopoeia

---

* *The Poems of Wilfred Owen*, edited with a Memoir by Edmund Blunden, Chatto & Windus, London, 1931, p.125. (See Part 5, Suggestions for further reading.)
† Paul Verlaine (1844–96), French symbolist poet whose poems are evocative rather than descriptive. The above remark was made in Blunden's Memoir in his edition of *The Poems of Wilfred Owen*, p.10. (See Part 5, Suggestions for further reading.)

of stanza 4 suggests agony and gasps for air: their/there/air, moans/ men, wry/Writhing. In his postcard to Leslie Gunston, Owen replies to his criticism of the pararhymes: 'I suppose I am doing in poetry what the advanced composers are doing in music. I am not satisfied with either.' We thereby understand that though Owen was attempting to express new and terrible experiences by new and disonant rhymes, he was still uncertain as to their effectiveness. ('From my Diary, July 1914' clearly shows that pararhyming is not intrinsically sombre.)

NOTES AND GLOSSARY:

Frond: leaf of a fern

fawns: deer; many editors think that Owen meant to write 'fauns' (Classical rural gods with horns and tail) but the introduction of classical mythology in this poem seems inappropriate to this writer

wry: distorted, turned to one side, grimacing. A particularly apt choice of word

shard: literally: fragment of pottery, here simply meaning fragment

amber: orange fossil resin used for ornaments, jewellery. Again, a particularly apt word—the orange glow of the firelight is like a luxurious fossil jewel for the oblivious future generations whose comfort was assured by the fossil coal and by what it symbolises (the miners and the soldiers) in the poem

ember: small pieces of fuel in a dying fire

Insensibility

Written sometime between October 1917 and January 1918, this Pindaric ode (a long lyric poem, serious in style with each stanza having its own pattern of varying line lengths, number of lines and rhyme scheme) was probably revised in April 1918 and may have been a reply to Wordsworth's ode 'Character of the Happy Warrior'. It follows the 'beatus ille' formula of Horace which became the English poetic cliché 'Happy the man who . . . ' in pastoral or didactic poetry of the seventeenth and eighteenth centuries. The form also echoes the beatitudes of the Sermon on the Mount (see Matthew 5: 1–12). Owen used it ironically, as he used other established poetic forms, to illustrate the great gap between life as we had hitherto known it and its horrific new aspect since the start of the World War. It is a restatement of Owen's almost obsessive theme of the gulf between soldiers and non-combatants. It is one of his few pararhymed poems, with a sparse and free pattern in keeping with its other irregularities. These allow a variation in pace which gives a spontaneous tone, an impression of a man thinking out loud.

The poem describes the effect of psychic numbing caused by the traumas of the war and compares this with the quite different numbness or insensibility of those who do not care enough about the fate of the·soldiers. Owen describes the various ways in which the soldiers have been rendered insensible. In the first stanza, it is soldiers who have suffered so much that they no longer feel compassion for their comrades. The stanza then attacks heroic poets who romanticise war: 'The front line withers./But they are troops who fade, not flowers'; the recruiting drives: 'Man, gaps for filling' (war posters had shown gaps in ranks of soldiers with the caption, 'Fill up the Ranks!'); and the euphemistic language of civil servants: 'Losses', that is, the needless dead. The second stanza deals with the soldiers who have even lost feeling for themselves. There is great irony in the 'tease and doubt of shelling'—language suitable for describing flirtation and not bombardment (compare 'S.I.W.'). The third stanza deals with those who are unable to use their imagination: they forget their past sufferings, they do not notice death and bleeding and their hearts, once constricted by terror, remain small and compassionless. Stanza 4 deals with soldiers on leave who can forget their experiences, or with the soldiers whose untrained minds allow them to forget what is happening. Stanza 5 turns to the poets, 'We wise', who feel too much: 'with a thought besmirch/Blood all over our soul'. How can they write their poetry?—only by learning the insensibility of the common soldier. The last stanza curses the 'dullards', that is, those who have never experienced battle and who cannot sympathise with the soldiers. They have made themselves immune to Owen's single most important quality: pity, the only appropriate response to the soldier's plight and to 'whatever moans in man', that is, all that is tragic in the human condition.

This poem reveals an aspect of Owen's vision of his role as a war poet. Though he saw a great gulf between soldiers and civilians, as most of his war poems reveal, he also saw a gulf between soldiers and officers, and in that respect was quite conventional in his views. Only a sense of superiority based on received notions of class and education could produce the lines: 'Happy the lad whose mind was never trained:/His days are worth forgetting more than not', while only an overriding empathy could prescribe the imaginative leap necessary to understand the true meaning of war: 'How should we see our task/But through his blunt and lashless eyes?'. The true dullards are not the uneducated common soldiers, but those, regardless of class, who make themselves immune to pity. However, the poem still leaves the impression of a sharp division between three estates: the common soldier, 'we wise', and the 'cursed ... dullards' which places the poet in a missionary and intercessory role.

NOTES AND GLOSSARY:

fleers: causes to make grimaces

alleys cobbled with their brothers: Owen wrote on 25 March 1918: 'They are dying again at Beaumont Hamel, which already in 1916 was cobbled with skulls.'* A cobblestone is one suitable for paving roads

shilling: newly recruited soldiers used to be paid the 'king's shilling'

cautery: the operation of cauterising, that is, burning with a hot iron for medical treatment, the side-effect of which might be permanent numbness

ironed: here, 'hardened'

taciturn: silent and dour

besmirch: soil, smear

reciprocity of tears: weeping in turn

Exposure

This poem refers to Owen's experiences of trench warfare during the unusually hard winter of early 1917. Though first drafted in December 1917, it was completed in September 1918 and is therefore among the last of his poems. It is listed under 'Description' in his Contents. It was inspired by Keats's 'Ode to a Nightingale' (lines 1–2: 'My heart aches, and a drowsy numbness pains/My senses') in which a mysterious union between nature and the poet is celebrated. The allusion may in part be ironic; the Romantics' optimistic view of nature is rejected by Owen because of his war experiences. His nature in 'Exposure' is a bleak concept of hostility and murderous cold, mirroring the behaviour of mankind in the war. The old idea of nature's benevolence does occur, but only in the soldiers' dreams.

Owen's use of the Romantic idiom is a translation of its painful eroticism, consumption and early death into the sufferings and violent death of trench warfare. Irony may well play a slighter role than claimed by most recent critics and interpreters of Owen. Often Keats seems too well absorbed and accepted to be used with irony, rather his attitudes and idioms are almost instinctively applied by Owen to his own circumstances. These circumstances of war happen to echo those of Keats who was well aware of his own impending death, but they are on quite a new scale of terror unknown to the Romantic poet. Indeed it is apparent that Owen is limited by the Romantic idiom which cannot fully accommodate the grotesqueness and barren horror of modern warfare. 'Exposure' is one of his few impressions of the landscape of war,

* *Collected Letters*, p.542.

and is perhaps the nearest he comes to modernism in its bleak imagery. It remains nevertheless laden with the Romantic richness from the poet's emotional response and his sensuous perception. (See discussion of irony and modernism in Part 3, p.63.)

The poem is set at the front line at night. Everything around the soldiers confuses and worries them. Nature's icy wind and snow, and the sights and sounds of war which fill her air—flares, gunnery rumbles, and whistling bullets—are harbingers of death. It is as if the war and nature were joined in one single hostile force. In this way the poem is universal, applying to no particular side in the war—except for the colour reference (grey) to the dawn (lines 13 and 14) whose army is thereby likened to the Germans. Amid these hostilities 'nothing happens', except the soldiers' dying. Stanza 5 modulates through one set of pararhymes (snow-dazed/sun-dozed) from the freezing present, the death by exposure, to the hallucination of the warmth of home. But even the soldiers' homes are empty and they are locked out, and so they have to return to the reality of their dying. Stanza 7 makes a faltering attempt at justifying their own deaths. It is to protect their hearths, their children and their land (though the syntactic elision of line 32 obscures its sense and the earlier drafts of the poem do not reveal any clearer meaning). The use of 'since', 'for', and 'therefore' implies a logical argument that is in fact not there. Nevertheless it is one of the few statements Owen made in his poems (for instance, in 'Greater Love' and 'At a Calvary near the Ancre'—see Part 3, p.68–9), that soldiers die like Christ as a sacrifice for others. At the same time he satirises this belief in 'Inspection', while in 'Strange Meeting' and 'Spring Offensive' he presents the soldier as the opposite of a Messiah, sacrificed to no purpose and damned without hope. Owen is full of such inconsistencies. His primary urge to write is based on strong feeling, not on reasoning. Stanza 7 continues with the idea that the soldiers fear God's order and love because he has permitted their condition to come about. They are therefore not reluctant to die, as many of them will that night, their eyes frozen like their spirits. We are left with the terrible image of a shivering group of soldiers burying their half-recognised comrades.

It may be that the argument that the soldiers' sacrifice is required for the sake of home, children and regeneration is not meant to be accepted by the reader and that there is an irony in the repeated line 'But nothing happens'. Something *is* happening: the soldiers are dying of exposure. If Owen's thinking is a little muddled in stanza 7, it well suits the confused thinking of dying men.

In common with Keats's poem, Owen's diction and imagery are expansive, but to new effect. The languor of Keats is turned to monotony in the line lengths, enforced four times by inconclusive lines (lines

1, 2, 3 and 11). By this and other devices the whole tone of the poem echoes the refrain 'But nothing happens'. However, the movement of the poem is not smooth; it falters in its slowness: inverted feet and ana- paestic* substitutions create a stumbling effect, as in lines 8 and 9. In fact, of the thirty-two lines of the poem, only five are metrically regu- lar. The tension between speech rhythms and the metrical pattern helps to convey an impression of disquiet. In line 12 several spondaic† or evenly stressed feet give onomatopoeic effect to the repetitive events described there. Lines 4 and 16 have repeated 's' sounds, imitating the sounds of whispering and of whistling bullets respectively. However, in the critical analysis of poetical devices, it should be borne in mind that speech sounds are relatively limited in comparison with natural sounds and that onomatopoeia is only latent in language and needs some key word to release this imitative potential. Obviously in lines 4 and 16 the key words are 'whisper' and 'bullets'. The pararhymes or approximate end-rhymes, many subtle, and not mere monosyllabic assonances, add intensity to the pervading tone of insecurity and anxiety (for example, silence/nonchalance). A perfect rhyme would be too predictable and reliable; the rhyme approximations confirm aurally that nothing is cer- tain except uncertainty. Occurring at widely spaced intervals they also add to the drawn-out melancholy of the poem. In all, the poem con- tains fine experiments with metre, onomatopoeia and rhythm that emphasise a nightmarish scene of alienation.

NOTES AND GLOSSARY:

salient: the part of the front line closest to enemy territory was called a 'salient'. At these points the fighting was intense. Otherwise the word is used to mean 'important'. Owen is obviously using it in both senses

nonchalance: (*French*) unconcern, listlessness

glozed: Owen's composite word from 'glowing' and 'glazed'

Slowly our ghosts drag home: see letter of 4 February 1917 to his mother, 'I thought of you and Mary without break all the time'

---

* Anapaest: a metrical foot of two unstressed and one stressed syllable. It is often used to create an impression of swiftness.
† Spondee: a metrical foot of two long or stressed syllables. Used occasionally to slow down the rhythm of a line for special effect.

The Show

Owen's experiences in battle during the first month of 1917 were the inspiration of this visionary poem. In his letter to his mother of 19 January 1917 he describes No Man's Land in these terms: 'pock-marked like a body of foulest disease and its odour is the breath of cancer . . . like the face of the moon chaotic, crater-ridden, uninhabitable, awful, the abode of madness'.* On 14 May 1917, he described to his brother Colin a shell attack after which 'the ground [was] all crawling and wormy with wounded bodies'.† At least two literary inspirations may be identified, Laurent Tailhade's lecture *Pour La Paix* (published in 1909) and Henri Barbusse's *Under Fire* (1917). Both these sources refer to worm-like crawling soldiers. The poem was written in November 1917 and revised in May 1918. Its epigraph, the quotation from W.B. Yeats which heads the poem, is taken from Forgael's speech in Yeats's play *The Shadowy Waters* (published 1906) and contains a Freudian slip (a mistake of Owen's appropriate to the poem but not to the play) — 'tarnished mirror' should read 'burnished mirror'. The artistic effectiveness of this epigraph in relation to the poem seems dubious. It is probably intended to be a condensed ironic allusion to Romantic poeticism, rather as other of his war poems allude ironically and more expansively to this poetic tradition in their form and content (for example, 'Greater Love', 'Exposure', and 'Apologia'). However, it cannot be said that the intended illumination sparked by the tension between the concerns of Romanticism and Owen's concern at the horror of war is achieved on the basis of this quotation; the poem succeeds on its intrinsic merits alone. It is an apocalyptic and hallucinatory insight into the 'Horrible Beastliness of War' (under which heading it is listed in Owen's Contents).

The Romantic tradition of the poet's isolation is in this poem translated into splendid detachment. The poet is elevated and sees the world 'from a vague height' in the company of Death. (Compare the imagery in 'O World of many Worlds', p.24.) From above he sees the desolate landscape of war which is like the face of a dead man whose beard is made of the barbed-wire defences, whose pockmarks and scabs are shell-holes and on whom grey and brown caterpillars are crawling, the German and British armies respectively. Added to this horrific and disgusting vision is the foul smell of the wounded and infested landscape. The armies of caterpillars are 'migrants from green fields, intent on mire', a clear allusion to the soldiers' journey from home to the

---

* *Collected Letters*, p.429
† Ibid., p.458.

battlefields. To make matters worse, Owen sees the enemy worms as more abundant and as devouring the rest. Terrified, the poet falls, as in a nightmare, to the ground where Death picks up a worm and shows him that its body is the men of Owen's platoon and that its freshly severed head is his own. The extended metaphor has been brought to an unexpected close and the identification of the poet with the landscape gives the poem a new emotional force. The poet was incriminated himself; he is not only a victim of the war, but amongst those responsible for perpetrating it. The *doppelgänger* theme (a man meeting his ghostly double) with its connotations of guilt is a peculiarly apposite symbol for the soldier as both slayer and victim.

The poem is not divided into stanzas as such, but into sentences, most of which form couplets. A similar freedom of form is used in the rhyme scheme. The pararhymes are sometimes widely and irregularly placed (for instance, feather/further, hid/head) and are less obtrusive than in his earlier experiments with this device (Compare 'Has your Soul Sipped?'). The metrical pattern is often broken to give the lines the rhythm of speech, and the juxtaposition of formality and informality adds to the impression of chaos. (Compare 'Exposure' and 'Spring Offensive'.) Some key words, 'sad' (line 3) and 'grey' (line 4), are emphasised by means of metrical deviation and by assonance and alliteration.

In the intensity and foulness of its imagery, this poem must be one of the most horrific war poems ever written in the English language. D.S.R. Welland (see Part 5, Suggestions for further reading) compares it with the war paintings of Paul Nash (1889–1946), some of which can be seen in the Tate Gallery, London.

NOTES AND GLOSSARY:

dearth:	scarcity of food, famine
brown ... grey:	British soldiers wore brown (khaki) uniforms, the Germans grey
mire:	swampy, muddy ground
Ramped:	an echo from Laurent Tailhade's *Pour la Paix*: 'Des larves rampent sur le sol' (literally: some grubs crawl on the ground)

Futility

This poem was written at Ripon in May 1918 and is listed under 'Grief' in Owen's *Table of Contents* together with 'Anthem for Doomed Youth'. It was published in *The Nation*, June 1918 (see Part 1, p.19). It is a famous and much adulated poem echoing Tennyson's *In Memoriam* 'O life as futile, then, as frail!' (lvi). It depicts a dead soldier, a country man whom the sun is unable to waken, as it awakens the seeds in the ground. Was man created for dying, the poem asks, and if so, what is the purpose of creation? The first difficulty raised in the poem is the role of the sun. It is of course a poetic and Romantic convention: the sun is the life-giver and as such a substitute for a moral as well as a creative force. As the poem ends with an angry accusation, the poem's best and most famous line: 'Was it for this the clay grew tall?', the sun seems, apart from its poetic conventionality, also to have a tactful role of deflecting criticism from a more usual or appropriate moral figure, that of God. That this coyness is not wholly successful, poetically as well as morally, can be understood when we first consider the absurd astronomy of line 9, (the earth was not a 'cold star' warmed by the sun), and secondly the connected and astonishing implication that mankind is an effect of the sun, and is therefore not autonomously responsible, and, to continue logically, not responsible for the war. This lends a curious impotency to the grief of lines 10–15. It belongs to the emotional order of a small boy stamping his foot against forces that seem beyond his control or influence. Hardly an appropriate response of a fighting man to war. Linked with the absurd astronomy, is the beginning of the poem—the strange suggestion that the dead man should be moved into the sun. The riddle of these connections is solved when the poem is seen in the light of an elaborate conceit about the sun, which takes over the whole meaning of the poem and, herein the poem's weakness, prevents any development in its brief compass of a proper understanding of the theme of the title: futility. The climax of the poem lies in no more than the suns's inability to awaken the soldier's dead limbs which makes the poet rail against the creation of life. This scene tells us nothing of the reason for his death. Here is an example of Owen not applying the precepts of his Preface. There is too much 'poetry' in this poem, too elaborate and inapposite a conceit which crowds out the 'pity' or the real thought and insights that might have been achieved.

But the poem has a studied elegance. It is composed of a series of hinted antitheses: man and Nature, futility and purposeful endeavour, past and present, creation and destruction. Its general tone is quiet, grave and impersonal—there is no mention of the war, no mention of bloodshed, no specific incident or place on which to focus, apart from an idea of winter. While this lends itself to a serious impersonality, and in the eyes of the poem's defenders, to a universality, to its detractors it could just as easily be seen as vague, over-generalised and dangerously unfocussed on its central subject. The futility of war lies in man's brutality towards man; the sun does not enter into this question. Owen has allowed his consideration of futility to be overshadowed by his choice of imagery. Coupled with the impersonality or vagueness, there is simplicity of diction: most of the words are monosyllables. In the falling cadences of his typical movement of vowel sounds from a higher to a lower pitch, there is an unobtrusive melancholy, ('Move him into the sun' and 'The kind old sun will know'). In the last line 'To break earth's sleep at all?' the sounds and rhythm lengthen and level out to bring the poem to a gentle and, in the musical sense, formally apt conclusion.

The metrical pattern (iambic lines, first and last of each stanza with three feet, intervening ones with four feet; an 'hourglass' in metric shape, as wittily described by F.W. Bateson*) is developed to allow a smooth regularity for the reflectiveness of stanza 1, while the emotional climax of the expostulation in stanza 2 is created by a series of adjectival phrases and rhetorical questions, slowing the movement and bringing the accusatory question of line 12 with its metrical regularity to a full prominence after the hesitancy of the preceeding lines. Mingled with this careful metrical structure is the regular pattern of mixed pararhymes and full rhymes, adding to its polished as well as musical impact. Formally, the poem is remarkable. There seems to have been more effort put into this aesthetic side than into any thought or idea which might have been its original impetus. The concluding impression is that the dead man is a stage-prop required for a polished poetic conceit. In the light of this poem, Yeats's rejection of war as a poetic subject becomes more understandable; if a poet's response to trench warfare is primarily one of elegant writing, then war becomes reduced to an aesthetically desirable poetic entity, like a flower.

NOTES AND GLOSSARY:
fatuous: foolish, silly

Strange Meeting

Fundamentally this poem shares its main theme with the previous poem, 'Futility', but its range of vision is far greater. Owen places it under the heading of 'Foolishness of War' in his Table of Contents. It was conceived over several months, incorporating fragments and drafts from November 1917 and was probably finished in the spring of 1918. Its literary origins and echoes are many, but it is also based on personal experiences—the night-time bombing raid in London,† the 1902 holiday in Ireland,** his sheltering for two days in a hole on the battlefield which eventually left him shell-shocked, and the images of the trenches themselves. The main literary source is Dante

---

* 'The Analysis of Poetic Texts: Owen's "Futility" and Davie's "The Garden Party"', *Essays in Criticism* (Oxford), April 1979, vol. 29, pp.156–164.
† Letter to Susan Owen (1 February 1916) in *Collected Letters*, p.377.
** Jon Stallworthy, *Wilfred Owen: A Biography*, Oxford University Press, London, 1974, p. 25.

Alighieri's (1268–1321) *Divina Commedia*, the section on the *Inferno* (Hell), especially the meeting between Dante and Ser Brunetto in Canto XV. The theme of this book of *The Commedia* is, as in Owen's poem, that of hopelessness and pity. The second major source is Shelley's *the Revolt of Islam*, Canto V, where an unexpected encounter in battle leads to a sudden realisation that all men are brothers. But Shelley's realisation is reached facilely and is over-optimistic, while Owen's is reached at great cost, and his version can be seen as a critical response to the Romantic view of war. There is also an echo of Keats's *The Fall of Hyperion* where truth is perceived by the sight of the suffering face of Moneta. Oscar Wilde's (1856–1900) *A Ballad of Reading Gaol* was quoted in one of the 1917 versions of the poem, and, while Wilde's poem is not directly referred to in this its final version, there are still echoes here of the ballad about a man who 'had killed the thing he loved/ And so he had to die'. In Henri Barbusse's *Le Feu*, Chapter XXI, the images of the casualty trench remind one of the groaning 'encumbered sleepers', as do the scenes from Sassoon's 'The Rear-Guard'.

Owen's poem is a dramatisation of the irresolvable conflict of his life as a poet/pacifist and officer/patriot. By making the object of his encounter one of the enemy, he has removed all possibility of a consolatory motif and has heightened the impossibility of his own position and the pity and absurdity of war. It is a deeply pessimistic and disillusioned poem, though Owen, through his frequent use of literary allusions, seems to derive some comfort from his literary precursors.

The poem commences as a visionary description, a dream of death, where the sonorous vowels of the second line echo as if from the granite tunnel itself and this eeriness is maintained throughout the poem by means of its pararhyming couplets. The great number of metrically unstressed syllables in this line receive a strong speech stress (spondees*) that leads to the plodding descent into Hell of line 4. When the sleeper springs up the tempo quickens; nearly all the syllables in lines 6 and 7 have short vowels and allow a number of tripping anapaestic* substitutions. The sleeper is suffering but loving, 'Lifting distressful hands, as if to bless'. Away from the battle, the poet naively comforts him, there is no cause for sorrow. The sleeper's answer makes it clear that he is the poet's *alter ego*, his better self: 'Whatever hope is yours,/ Was my life also.' He mourns because of the waste of his years—for the pursuit not of romantic love, but of poetic truth which conquers time (and therefore death)—'But mocks the steady running of the hour'. Through his art he might have taught grief, joy and truth—above all truth about the pity of war. But now, because he is silenced in death, men will, without the benefit of his art, continue with 'what we

* See footnotes, p.47.

spoiled', that is, with the war, for which, by the use of the pronoun 'we', the speaker takes his share of responsibility. In a prophetic vision of the future, the sleeper sees that nations will regress, abandon progress and become totalitarian, 'None will break ranks'. (Compare 'O World of Many Worlds'; individualism was for Owen the salvation of the human spirit, and he took an apocalyptic view of the effects of the war which was not far from historical reality.) The sleeper possessed the courage and wisdom to avoid the mass movement towards disaster, into 'vain citadels that are not walled', that is, into the metaphorical bastions of national prejudice. He would have been able to undo the harm of war, wash the blood-clogged wheels of the chariots with truth drawn from the unpolluted waters of what is finest and deepest in the human spirit. But this would not have been done by fighting. He would have given as much through his art—'Foreheads of men have bled where no wounds were', a reference to the suffering of Christ, the implication being that one can suffer as much through art or by dedicating one's life to the distillation of truth, as one can suffer through 'the cess of war'.

The last five lines confront us with Owen's share of guilt; he has slain the sleeper, his mirrored self—the poet from the enemy's side, and is confronted by him in Hell. With the best of the world slain, the future for the living is bleak, and the best, having blood on their hands, are condemned at least to an everlasting sleep. The reader is left without hope. The *Doppelgänger* theme—the confrontation with oneself after death—is appropriate to Owen's dichotomous position. The use of it in this wide-ranging but controlled vision of the impact of war focuses attention on the position of the creative artist who is also a soldier. It is a journey of an archetypal universality; the profound tunnel is also his own subconscious mind wherein he discovers the consequences of his involvement with the war as well as its impact on mankind. It is no accident that there are a great many literary influences and precedents underlining the universality of this poem, but it is also of all Owen's poems the most deeply revealing about his own role, that is, not about his character, but about the universal or impersonal side of himself. The poem is his own elegy; lines 15 to 39 are as if spoken by himself: 'I went hunting wild/After the wildest beauty in the world . . . I had mastery:/To miss the march of this retreating world.' The tragedy is that it is not a statement of what he had done, or what he intends to do, but of what he would have done. The romantic toying with easeful death has turned into a grim prophecy of his own, and indeed of other great poets', untimely death in a futile war.

NOTES AND GLOSSARY:

groined: scooped out (from 'groin', the depression or fold on both sides of the body between the upper thigh and the abdomen)

probed:	this image echoes very closely Sassoon's 'The Rear-Guard' where the rear-guard tugs and kicks what he presumes to be a sleeping, but is actually a dead soldier in a trench, in order to get a reply
grained:	lined, as the pattern in wood

The Sentry

Owen based this poem on a specific incident at the front line in January 1917, described in a letter to his mother of 16 January of that year.* He began writing it at Craiglockhart in the autumn of 1917, revised it in May 1918, and finished it in France in September 1918, only a few weeks before his death.

In this poem Owen describes with stark realism one of his 'unsurpassable' experiences, unmitigated by poetic allusions, myths or meditative passages. Apart from the richness of the colloquially realistic and descriptive language, in this poem he is approaching the subject in a manner similar to Sassoon and Rosenberg. 'The Dead-Beat', 'S.I.W.', 'Disabled' and possibly 'Dulce Et Decorum Est' belong to this category of his writing. In their concreteness, these poems are part of a slowly growing general movement towards greater realism in poetry in the years before the war. This trend was already noticeable in the writings of W.B. Yeats, John Masefield (1878–1967), and J.M. Synge (1871–1909), whose dictum has become a critical slogan for the movement: 'before verse can be human again it must learn to be brutal' (from Preface to *Poems and translations*, 1909).

The poem is a vivid and dramatic description of how one man becomes a casualty of trench warfare. While 'Dulce Et Decorum Est'

---

* 'My dug-out held 25 men tight packed. Water filled it to a depth of 1 or 2 feet, leaving say 4 feet of air.

One entrance had been blown in and blocked. So far, the other remained.

The Germans knew we were staying there and decided we shouldn't.

Those fifty hours were the agony of my happy life.

Every ten minutes of Sunday afternoon seemed an hour.

I nearly broke down and let myself drown in the water that was now slowly rising over my knees.

Towards 6 o'clock, when, I suppose, you would be going to church, the shelling grew less intense and less accurate: so that I was mercifully helped to do my duty and crawl, wade, climb and flounder over No Man's Land to visit my other post. It took me half an hour to move about 150 yds . . .

In the Platoon on my left the sentries over the dug-out were blown to nothing. One of these poor fellows was my first servant whom I rejected. If I had kept him he would have lived, for servants don't do Sentry Duty. I kept my own sentries half way down the stairs during the more terrific bombardment. In spite of this one lad was blown down and, I am afraid, blinded.

This was my only casualty' (*Collected Letters*, p.428).

builds up to an exclusive concentration on the individual's agony and insists that the reader cannot understand it, the focus in 'The Sentry' is blurred. The blinded man is forgotten in the confusion of battle and multiple affliction, and only in *dreaded* memories and dreams is his plight remembered by the poet. The emotions conjured by this poem are wider-ranging and more compassionate than the impatient indignation and moralising of 'Dulce Et Decorum Est'.

The incident is clear enough: while Owen is sheltering with his men during shelling in a flooded dug-out, the sentry, keeping a look-out from the top of the steps to its entrance, is blown down the stairs in a deluge of mud and debris. He is blinded, and though Owen sends for a stretcher and briefly tries to comfort him, he forgets him, distracted by his duties of posting another sentry and setting off in the mud to check his other dug-out. He is, however, later haunted in dreams by the image of the sentry's blasted eyes and by his delirious and deluded shout before he is carried off that he can see light.

The diction is not poetic in the romantic sense. It is, however, richly descriptive in its use of slang and colloquialisms, nearly all of which have unpleasant connotations: 'frantic', 'slime', 'slush', 'murk', 'thump', 'wretches', 'crumps', 'spew', 'pummel', and so on. There are notably few adjectives and a great number of onomatopoeic participles: 'guttering', 'thumping', 'sploshing', 'buffeting', 'snuffing', 'flound'ring', and so on; onomatopoeic exclamations: 'thud! flump!'; and figurative use of verbs, 'herded', 'dredged', 'pummelled', 'slogged', and so on. The result is vivid. Owen uses alliteration and assonance with his customary abundance, and succeeds in infusing the poem with an emotional intensity that has a nightmarish quality, and occasionally an onomatopoeic force: 'And gave us hell, for shell on frantic shell'. That this incident and others like it were part of his shell-shock nightmares is clear not only from the general quality of this poem, and of 'Dulce Et Decorum Est', but from their specific reference to dreaded dreams (line 23; lines 15 and 16 in 'Dulce . . . '; see also line 6 in 'Greater Love'). The syntax of lines 13–15 creates dramatic tension through the delayed entrance of the sentry—his body, the subject of the verb, appears last in the clause, followed by the debris in the mud. In this passage the 'u' sound of 'buffeting' is echoed repeatedly in the following lines: 'snuffing', 'thud', 'flump', 'thumping', 'flood', 'muck', and so on, which, together with the irregularities of metre (especially in line 13) heighten the impression of noisy confusion. The rhyme scheme is loosely based on rhyming couplets, but is often broken and interspersed with pararhymes.

In common with all his other late poems ('Spring Offensive', 'Smile, Smile, Smile', 'Exposure'), it offers no comfort, no consolation for the suffering. It is a dark view: the lights had indeed 'long gone out'.

NOTES AND GLOSSARY:

whizz-bangs: high-velocity bombs that exploded almost as soon as they could be heard passing through the air

curse ... corpses: a near pun

herded: an echo of the first line of 'Anthem for Doomed Youth'

deluging: flooding

dredge: clean or fetch up from river or sea-bed

huge-bulged like squids: nightmarish sea image repeated from 'Dulce Et Decorum Est' (see lines 13–16). The double-barrelled adjective is a left-over from the luxurious diction of Keats. Even at his most stark, Owen is still under the influence of the Romantics

flound'ring: see Owen's letter of 16 January 1917, quoted in the footnote on p.54

spewed: vomited

And one who would have drowned himself for good: Owen himself. See his letter of 16 January 1917

crumps: (*slang*) hard hits; the word was also used to mean a small shell in the First World War

pummelled: literally: beat with the fists, usually repeatedly

slogged: (*slang*) punched, hit hard

Spring Offensive

Begun in July 1918 and finished in France during September of that year, the poem draws on Owen's experiences of the Allies' 'spring offensive' in April 1917. However, these experiences are translated onto a universal and impersonal plane; it is a war poem written at a year's distance from the action.

The title epitomises the conflict that the poem embodies: the unnatural offence of war against nature. In both this poem and 'Strange Meeting' Owen considers the relationship between war and poetry, and the insoluble dilemma of the soldier poet. It is written in the tone and style of a pastoral idyll and in its first two stanzas draws considerably on two of Keats's Odes, 'To a Nightingale' and 'To Autumn'. The 'ease' of the insensible of stanza 1, those who can sleep, as opposed to those who stay awake realising the import of the occasion, is not only a borrowed image from Owen's own poem 'Insensibility', but is also an apposite borrowing from 'Ode to a Nightingale' where the poet has toyed with the idea of 'easeful Death'. The inversion of 'Marvelling they stood' (line 7) echoes 'Darkling I listen' from the sixth stanza of 'To a Nightingale', again relating to death. The May breeze, 'murmurous with wasp and midge' reverberates stanza 5 of Keats's poem ('And mid-May's eldest child,/The coming musk-rose, full of dewy wine,/ The murmurous haunt of flies on summer eves'), enriching by this literary association the sense of nature's warmth and plenty as well as the frightening transience of life. Similarly, 'the summer oozed into their veins' in line 9, and 'Hour after hour' in line 13, echo directly 'Thou watchest the last oozings hours by hours' of 'Ode to Autumn'. Owen's uses of these references are complex. They are on the one hand supports and inspirations, a familiar idiom which gives him confidence to tackle his bewilderingly new subject of war. There is perhaps, on the other hand, some irony in his use of them, though this is less apparent in 'Spring Offensive' than in his other poems. His despair *is* a greater emotion than the melancholy of Keats which, however, is less trivial than Owen's ironies in his earlier poems might allow, for Keats's melancholy is no mere pose and is based on the idea of transience, disease, pain and early death, set against the glory of nature and the permanence of art. Owen's response is on an entirely new scale, but still parallel to Keats's response, for it is undoubtedly based on horror of death, love of nature and respect for art. War, however, has distorted events to such an extent that Owen takes an *apocalyptic* view of the relationship between man and nature. The scale is that of the Second Fall, 'the end of the world', as the poem states. In the post-Craiglockhart poems in which he takes a general view of the war (that is, where the subject of the poem is not confined to a particular incident or individual), and which are considered by most critics to be his finest poems, he steps straight from his earlier romantic idylls into these pastoral nightmares without an attempt at what could be called realism. Realism in Owen is confined to his colloquial poems inspired by Sassoon which tackle confined and immediate problems of individuals in which nature plays little part, and they seem in the total of his work more like a temporary digression than a part of his central idiom. In Owen's poetry of the modern apocalypse ('The Show', 'Exposure', 'Strange Meeting', and 'Spring Offensive'), his diction, poetic conventions and reformist fervour remain firmly rooted in Romantic traditions, while his images from the war are new and horrifying. In 'Spring Offensive' they are the landscape of trench warfare, 'the imminent line of grass'; the injected drug; the new sky of terrifying flashes and of the mysterious ominous impersonality of 'glass'; and a nature that has become the very brink of hell. The sky in Owen's poetry has become a symbol of hostility, like the hostile dawn in 'Exposure' and 'Mental Cases', just as the sun itself is the creative principle from which the soldiers have cut themselves off, 'The sun, like a friend with whom their love is done.' (Compare the creative sun in 'Futility'.)

Stanza 3 continues with his Romantic and familiar references. He uses an image from his childhood: 'Had blessed with gold their slow boots coming up'*, and the traditional pathetic fallacy†of plants trying to restrain the men from their deeds. But so long as the soldiers remain contemplating nature, they are part of nature themselves and 'breathe like trees unstirred'. But when, in stanza 4, they move into battle, they break the bond with nature by a look in their face—a look that would tell a lover that their relationship is over (lines 23 and 24). It is also a look that is more powerful than the sun—an ominous and mysterious line successfully developed from the bathetic conclusion of his early 'O World of many Worlds'. It seems that man's iniquity is a force greater than beneficent nature's, a view understandable when one considers the total destruction represented by a battlefield. With a sense of natural justice and poetic tact, Owen forgets in his war poetry nature's relentless ability to regenerate.

In stanza 5 the soldiers race (compare this with the slow pace of the previous stanzas) to the battle, where the notable position of 'Exposed' in line 29 emphasises their vulnerability in the landscape. As they move, thus singled out, what seems to be the whole of nature, or at least its hostile side symbolised by the sky, bursts into a fury of attack against them. The enemy is transmuted onto this universal plane. The whole poem is in fact an impersonal account; the enemy is not mentioned, the soldiers not identified, and as in his other war poems, 'Futility' and 'Exposure', the setting is made no more specific than by the time of year. The impersonality of the attack is sustained throughout the rest of the poem where it is described with formal unity and control in terms of the landscape and nature already described in the earlier stanzas. The buttercups (or pits in the ground) become the sacrificial chalices that catch the soldiers' blood, and the horizon becomes the edge of the world, the sheer chasm down which the soldiers may fall to their deaths. The image of the sacrifice is continued in stanza 6 where in 'that last high place', the high altar of Golgotha, the soldiers are felled by bullets or blown up by shells likened to the blasting heat of hell, or fall from the edge of the world. Owen introduces a calculated doubt into his moral indignation—'*Some say* God caught them' (italics mine)—not present in the impotent anger of 'Futility'.

But the conclusion of the poem (stanza 7) turns to the survivors, those who are still among us. The poem asks, what did they see and experience in 'hell', why do they not tell what happened? The answer lies in the preceding lines 'there out-fiending all its fiends and flames/

---

* See Harold Owen, *Journey from Obscurity*, Vol. I, Oxford University Press, London, 1963, p.165. Harold Owen's boots had been covered with buttercup petals when returning through fields to Shrewsbury after Evensong in Uffington Church. Wilfred Owen then told his family: 'Harold's boots are blessed with gold.'
† A phrase coined by Ruskin in 1856. Used now to describe the common poetic phenomenon of attributing human feelings to the inanimate.

With superhuman inhumanities,/Long-famous glories [a bitterly ironic comment on conventional attitudes to war], immemorial shames'. The survivors cannot speak for shame. This idea of shame, of the taint of war, was already tackled by Owen in his sonnet 'Happiness' written in February 1917: 'Have we not wrought too strange and sorrowful wrongs/For her hands' pardoning?... Yet heaven looks smaller than the old doll's home/... The former happiness is unreturning.' And later in 'The Send-Off' (Spring 1918): 'So secretly, like wrongs hushed-up, they went... /A few... May creep back, silent...'. It seems that those who have entered hell must be tainted for evermore with the knowledge of it. As Christopher Marlowe's (1564–93) Mephistopheles says in Faustus's study, 'Why, this is hell, nor am I out of it' (*Doctor Faustus*, I. 3).

'Spring Offensive' rests on several anthitheses: the unnaturalness of what men are doing/the natural background; the benevolence of nature/ the revenge of nature; death/life; relaxation/tension, and so on. These antitheses reinforce the sense of alienation in the poem produced by the soldiers' participation in the destruction, and sharply reflect the irrec-oncilable division between the soldier and poet in Owen's own soul.

NOTES AND GLOSSARY:

begird: belt themselves; figuratively, prepare themselves for action

his: (line 26) the sun's

sheer: this word appears in two letters of the period when the poem was written (to his mother, 4 October 1918, and to Sassoon, 10 October 1918). Reading between the lines of his description of dreams and fantasies, it is more than likely that his neurasthe-nic nightmares included repeated dreams of falling to his death

drave: (*archaic*) past participle of 'drive'

Part 3

Commentary

The Preface and Table of Contents

Owen started to draft a preface and table of contents for his collection of war poems, which was probably to be entitled *Disabled and Other Poems*, in May 1918. (See Part 1, p.17.) Both are incomplete and only exist in heavily corrected manuscript form. It is therefore difficult to draw any detailed conclusions about their content. It would also be fair to say that some of the statements made in the Preface, general and hasty as they seem, do not bear close scrutiny, especially, for example, the first two sentences: 'This book is not about heroes. English Poetry is not yet fit to speak of them,' and also the often quoted line 'Above all I am not concerned with Poetry.' From the analysis in Part 2 in these Notes, it should be clear that he *was* deeply concerned with the techniques and aesthetics of poetry writing. These statements become more understandable in the context of the mass of contemporary publications about the war, many from 'soldier poets', that echoed the politicians' belligerent and heroic speeches, and continued the Horatian poetic tradition of glory in war. This was the 'Poetry' with which Owen was not concerned, and it should be realised that he was among the very few who took such a negative view of the war.* He could perhaps have meant in his opening sentences that heroes in the Horatian sense were not a fit poetic subject, or that the heroes of the First World War were of such a new order that no adequate poetic response seemed to exist as yet. They were 'troops who fade, not flowers,/For poets' tearful fooling' ('Insensibility'). However, the general impression of the Preface is that, with its obscurities, it is a tactical smoke-screen to deflect any criticism that his poems were not celebratory. It avoids direct criticism of the Horatian tradition and of conventional attitudes while clarifying his own stance.

One of the keys to understanding his poetry lies in the famous centre lines: 'My subject is War, and the pity of War./The Poetry is in the pity.' It is clear that Owen saw a new purpose in his poetry once he had seen active service, and that this purpose was to expose the futile sufferings which war caused. At the time of writing the Preface at least, he

---

* Compare the artistic detachment of Yeats who was able to write of the 'terrible beauty ...born' out of the violence and murders of the 1916 Easter Rising in Ireland.

felt more concerned with the urgency and truth of this message than with the art of his poetry. There is a strong propagandist element in his work. However, Owen's talents did not lie in the direction of satire, a usual form for instigating social action and a mode used by Sassoon in his war poems. Owen's nature inclined him towards elegiac writing the function of which is to arouse grief and to stimulate remembrance. In this vein of poetry he found his models in Tennyson and Shelley. He investigated the poetic form of the elegy in his reading in late 1917 and 1918, including the classical sources of Shelley's famous lament for Keats, *Adonais*. Owen is usually at his best when the emotion of grief predominates over disgust in his poems and when tribute is paid to the men who died 'as cattle' rather than when criticism is directly made of the perpetrators of war. In his Preface, he referred to his poems as elegies, but they offer no consolation to his readers, serving instead to warn them of the true nature of war. This message is certainly discernible in the pessimism of his poems, normally encapsulated in the last line as a parting shot at the reader. Apart from his earliest attempts at war poetry, before his active service, there is not one war poem of his that does not express both pity and warning.

The closing paragraph of the Preface shows that, despite sustained attempts at neutrality and objectivity in his poetry, he was no friend of the Germans. He certainly feared what might have been the consequences of their victory. But unlike the last lines of his poems, he also hints in the Preface that the suffering of the dead might have had some value if future generations will learn from the spirit of his work.

The Table of Contents shows by its listing of the motives behind the poems that Owen meant to make a systematic survey of the nature of modern warfare and its effect upon civilians and soldiers alike. His poems were not just individual narratives or descriptive pieces, but they were to be part of a panoramic view. Each of the motives is calculated to inspire loathing of war; not one offers consolation or hope: even the motive of 'Cheerfulness' refers ironically to the poor joy that the men can wring out of the horror of the trenches.

Owen's poetry and the war

For reasons of space not more than a couple of poems from Owen's early, or pre-war, work have been considered in Part 2. However, from a study of these it is clear that he was a fervent and competent, though not a notable, follower of Romantic and late Victorian poetry. This was inevitable, given his choice of reading: Keats, Shelley, Tennyson, Swinburne and Wilde. In common with late Victorian writers of the aesthetic school, he had a strong interest in poetic form which he maintained until his death. Very early in his poetic career he became considerably skilled in a wide variety of the crafts of poetry: metrical forms, rhyme schemes, assonance, alliteration, a growing repertoire of imagery, the forms of odes, sonnets, narrative verse and so on, even if his treatment of his largely conventional subjects was immature, the product of ill-founded emotions, ill-conceived ideas and plain lack of experience. But his particular range of subject matter in his pre-war poems was nevertheless revealing in relation to his post-Craiglockhart poems. The pre-war poems deal with his role as a poet, his isolation in his vocation, fame and financial independence, as shown in his poems 'To Poesy', 'The Dread of Falling into Naught', 'O World of many Worlds', 'A Palinode', and 'Deep under turfy grass'. The last of these poems reveals too his rejection of orthodox religion, more fully expressed in 'Unto what pinnacles of desperate heights', completed shortly before he left the vicarage at Dunsden. His religious training, however, was later to be translated into a missionary and intercessory role on behalf of the common soldier, as 'Insensibility' reveals. His early poems also record his Keatsian quest for beauty in the face of passing time and human suffering, as illustrated in 'The Fates' and 'Stunned by their life's explosion into Love'. A few poems survive from this period that were written in a positive frame of mind to imaginary girl friends, 'Impromptu: I have none other thought of peace, but only Thee' and 'How do I love thee?', but many of his early love poems show a markedly ambivalent attitude towards women, for example, 'To the Bitter Sweet-Heart: A Dream'. Several reveal a greater interest in young men, for example, 'It was a navy boy', in children (of either sex) or in imaginary male figures symbolising the lure of the flesh and possibly some idea of a masculine and creative force, as in 'Storm' and 'The time was aeon'. In a poem not otherwise profoundly revealing, of unknown date, but probably pre-dating his army career, he wrote with an unrealised and prophetic accuracy: 'So I, lightly addressing me to love,/Have found too late love's grave significance' ('The Peril of Love'). In fact, he never found it before his death. It was fortunate that Keats and Shelley exerted a more profound influence on him than Swinburne and Wilde whose aestheticism did sometimes deteriorate into posturing affectation, insipid idealism and plain silliness, the latter quality well illustrated in Owen's decadent poem 'Has your Soul Sipped?' where the 'sweetness of all sweets' is the smile on the corpse of a boy with his throat cut. Keats taught him a richness of diction and the importance of sound in poetry, and also that the privileged few who were poets had the sacred task of searching for Beauty and Truth. But above all, Keats was the model of artistic selflessness that helped Owen develop his remarkable impersonality in his greatest war poems. Shelley showed him that the poet had a duty to work for peace and humanity; he was behind much of the moral certainty of Owen's later poetry.

The impact of the war on his work was immense, though it was delayed. It gave him a subject matter worthy of his emotional fervour and rich poetic idiom. His year of military training in 1916 was so busy that he had little time to write poetry. The terrible experiences of the battlefield of early 1917 which led to his neurasthenia also meant that his poetic production was less than prolific until the summer, and what there was, was still very much in the mode of his pre-war poems. It was the leisure of Craiglockhart and the guiding kindred spirit of Sassoon that helped him to find his voice to express the impact of the war on his poetry.

His by then well developed romantic idiom was peculiarly suited to the topic of suffering and death. The strong emotions and luxurious diction of Romanticism, and particularly of Romantic love poetry, are equally apposite to the expression of their extreme opposites, and the overtones of evil and sadism that are part of the decadence of Romanticism create an intensity and depravity of emotion that imbues the scenes of death and fighting with an iniquity not to be conveyed through colloquial or matter-of-fact idiom. References, direct or implied, to this great poetic tradition, and other references to past poets (for example, Dante in 'Strange Meeting' or 'Mental Cases') deepen the meaning of the poetry: if present subject matter is related to poetry of the past it takes on a significance that transcends the limitations of time and place. This universal emotional scale of his verse fits a world war.

Much of Owen's emotional intensity, however, is achieved through an irony which is complex in its action. Obviously the expectations of subject and mood aroused by the Romantic idiom do not at first sight include the devastations of modern warfare. The reader is shocked by the contrast. There is an implication in Owen's use of the Romantic style that no significant emotional experiences of the past hundred years can compare with the horrors of modern warfare. Certainly, according to Owen, love cannot compare with the experiences of warfare, as is shown in 'Greater Love' and 'Apologia Pro Poemate Meo'. The gulf between idiom and subject matter creates and simultaneously is a product of a deep sense of unreality and alienation (as in 'Strange Meeting' or 'Exposure'). This is perhaps the most remarkable quality of Owen's poetry. His continued use of a borrowed style might have relegated him to the category of pastiche, but the subject of war coupled with his Keatsian poetic impersonality, in that he avoids dealing with his personal sufferings and expresses the effects of the war on his fellow soldiers on a scale of universal significance, results in a poetry which has a modernistic aspect. It attempts, and often succeeds in coming to grips with a new consciousness produced by radical social, economic and political changes all of which caused a sense of strain, alienation and a feeling of lack of coherence. The anger Owen shows towards authority (military or religious), his repeatedly expressed view of the individual soldier as a victim, and his revulsion at the idea of romantic love in the face of the dying and maimed soldiers are three cases in point. This is an aspect of his poetry that has not been emphasised enough. Modernism is too often only associated with more radical and spectacular attempts to create new forms to express the new order of existence. Owen has illustrated, however, that it can find expression in traditional forms through an ironic relationship with them. Owen's use of irony then, is a profoundly significant part of his style, and should not be confused with the usual sophisticated mockery of events. It is, rather, as Stephen Spender has pointed out,* his acceptance of the irony of events which mock at poetry. Unlike Ezra Pound or T.S. Eliot he heralds no stylistic or theoretical revolution and does not intellectualise. His only formal innovation of rhyming through consonance is practised within established poetic structures which are, however, loosened by it, and, because of it, pervaded by a melancholic or minor tone.

The friendship with Sassoon was important for the confidence and contacts that it gave Owen, and for the influence of his colloquial style. Sassoon's anger at the unnecessary slaughter of the Somme and his determination to inform the complacent public of the real conditions at the front unleashed in Owen's verse his detestation of the war and helped to define the recurring 'two nations' theme in his poetry. It was as if he needed the permission of this maturer man to voice his minority view. Sassoon's influence was felt immediately, as can be seen in the startling contrast in both subject matter and style between 'Song of Songs' and 'The Dead-Beat'. Sassoon's colloquialisms and his remarks on Owen's 'embarrassing sweetness in the sentiment of some of his work' and 'over-luscious writing' helped to temper some of the latter's excesses. Written very obviously under the direct influence of Sassoon are 'The Letter', 'Dulce Et Decorum Est', 'The Chances', 'The Sentry', and 'Smile, Smile, Smile', their dates of composition showing that right up to his death Owen was deeply affected by Sassoon's style, but that the colloquialisms soon settled in his poems, and particularly well in his greatest poems, into becoming part of his essential and ironic contrasting of the Romantic idiom and with a modern or 'colloquial' subject. When Owen reflects Sassoon most directly, he is at his most strident and rhetorical (for example, in 'The Dead-Beat' and 'Dulce Et Decorum Est'). When Sassoon's influence is assimilated to become a linguistic echo or stylistic aberration (the startling 'thumped' of line 13 in 'Strange Meeting') or is simply present in the confidence with which Owen tackles the horror of warfare, Owen's poetry is at its best:

* In *The Struggle of the Modern*, Hamish Hamilton, London, 1963, p.169.

evoking pity in the traditional heightened style that was nevetheless rapidly becoming uniquely his. The two poems 'The Next War' and 'S.I.W.' clearly illustrate that he is not so much concerned with the fighting itself as with the values and processes which bring about fighting and how these are perceived and ironically assimilated by the soldiers. In 'The Next War' the soldiers are fighting for the wrong cause and comfort themselves with ironic bravado. In 'S.I.W.' ('Self-Inflicted Wound') the attitude of the soldier's family towards war is ridiculed. Here Owen presents us with the causes of war as well as its effects (the suffering of the soldier). Its causes are the superficiality and inadequacies of the family's understanding of such concepts as patriotism and disgrace, as well as a lack of understanding of what a wound really means, 'a nice safe wound to nurse', or of what support of a loved one really means, 'send his favourite cigarette'. This poem makes clear Owen's fundamental argument (never directly stated, but often implied) against the war: war is brought about by many minor slacknesses of thought, by small and easy self-indulgences and their culmination into a major evil is therefore a collective responsibility of the nation—only the soldier is absolved by Owen because of his suffering. And the worst of it is, that such collective attitudes are kept alive by lies; the Epilogue of 'S.I.W.' (more ironical than cynical) shows how the family learns nothing from the tragedy of the soldier's suicide. His last and perhaps greatest poem 'Spring Offensive' shows in its combination of fervent love of nature and life, by its theme of alienation from them through modern warfare, by its moral intensity, and by the universality of its poetic diction that his stated motive of pity has become quite oblique or indirect, and is, in its culmination of themes and idioms, a fitting finale to his work. These were the constructs of his elegies which show us that pity is the most important outcome of war, that truth does find expression and that his one voice of love rises above the hatred of total war.

Sassoon is also present in what seem to be Owen's two basic ways of viewing the war. When using Sassoon's voice most directly, Owen tends to examine particular cases of suffering as in 'The Dead-Beat', 'The Letter', 'Disabled', death in 'Dulce Et Decorum Est', 'The Chances', 'Inspection', 'S.I.W.', 'A Terre' and 'The Sentry'. He then takes a closer or more specific view of the war. When writing in his elegiac voice, influenced by all his poetic models, he takes a more distant view of the war, literally in the case of 'The Show' where his soul hovers over the earth, too much so in 'Futility' where his distancing produces a fatuous generality, and with a timeless and profound universality in 'Mental Cases', 'Strange Meeting' and 'Spring Offensive'. But whether his view is specific or distant, Owen regards the *survivors* of warfare with an insistent interest accorded by no other war poet. They are always mentally maimed, often physically as well. The lie of patriotism, the vanity of sexual pride reduces a strong boy to the grey institutionalised life of an old cripple in 'Disabled'. The horrors of warfare bleed men of all feeling in 'Insensibility', of love of life in 'Exposure', while the officer of 'A Terre' feels unable to house his soul. ˜he survivors of 'Spring Offensive' come back, in effect, mute, havin͓ ᴏeen rendered speechless by 'superhuman inhumanities'. But the survivors, 'whose minds the Dead have ravished', in the intensely horrific 'Mental Cases' embody the utmost of degradation and suffering in his poems.

Owen's imagery

Throughout his poetry Owen uses images of darkness and of sinking. Dreadful or appalling darkness occurs in the early 'On My Songs' and 'The Unreturning', and in the image of his poetic path in 'O World of many Worlds'. In his first poem on the outbreak of the war, '1914', 'perishing great darkness' becomes an image of war. It is possible that the 'dark' loneliness which is the sphere of the Romantic poet, had become the dark environment of war on which it was his duty to shed light:

> Glorious will shine the opening of my heart;
> The land shall freshen that was under gloom;
>
> 'Storm' (October 1916)

With his shell-shock in 1917 came images of sinking both in letters and in poems—the drowning of 'Dulce Et Decorum Est' and the drowning and 'flound'ring' of 'The Sentry'. Closely related to this feeling is the idea of submerging into the earth. 'Inspection', 'Asleep', 'A Terre' and 'Smile, Smile, Smile' all use this image. It culminates in the vision of an underground tunnel, developed from 'Miners' to the tunnel of hell in 'Strange Meeting' and later to a Dantesque inferno in 'Mental Cases'. Now that the chronology of his poems is known and we have their drafts, it is possible to discern a developing or deepening image of war as a cavernous hell in his late poems. The drafts of 'Exposure', and 'Cramped in that funnelled hole', reveal that the shell crater that will engulf the soldiers is the mouth of hell. In 'Mental Cases' the soldiers driven insane by the war are seen as damned souls actually in hell. In 'Strange Meeting', the soldier-poet himself is condemned to hell and himself makes the journey; war has silenced him as it has silenced the survivors of 'Spring Offensive' who have, however, managed to come back from 'this world's verge' of 'fiends and flames'.

Perhaps linked with these dark infernal images are Owen's other images of eyes and blinding ('The Sentry' and 'Dulce Et Decorum Est'), and his poems constructed round the cycle of night and day. 'The Calls' begins at dawn and ends at midnight; 'Song of Songs' and 'From

My Diary, July 1914' likewise close with nocturnal eroticism. Many of his war poems refer to the destructive power of dawn and the deadliness of night:

> Sunlight seems a blood-smear; night comes blood-black;
> Dawn breaks open like a wound that bleeds afresh.
>
> 'Mental Cases' (May 1918)

The young soldier in 'S.I.W.' commits suicide at dawn. The whole of the fragment 'I saw his round mouth's crimson' compares death with a sunset and the fall of night. 'Exposure' is set in the 'poignant misery of dawn' which is as much an enemy and killer as the Germans, 'massing in the east her melancholy army' and attacking 'once more in ranks on shivering ranks of gray'. But the sun itself is beneficent, as in 'Futility' and 'Spring Offensive' where it is in turn 'kind' and 'like a friend'. In 'Happiness' it cleanses human wrong-doing. This is not necessarily an inconsistency; the cool of dawn is universally associated with death when the human metabolism is running at its lowest, the 'weak-limned hour when sick men's sighs are drained' ('The Unreturning'); the warm sun of the day is obviously a life-giver; and these two opposite views fit Owen's ambivalent view of nature. Nature is a source of aesthetic joys ('From My Diary, July 1914'), the cycle of life ('1914'), but she is ravaged and degraded by war ('The Show') and therefore wreaks vengeance:

> ... And instantly the whole sky burned
> With fury against them; earth set sudden cups
> In thousands for their blood; and the green slope
> Chasmed and steepened sheer to infinite space.
>
> 'Spring Offensive'

Here the whole landscape, which had been benign—warm and loving, blessing the soldiers' boots, clinging to them to stop the warfare (in the image of the brambles)—turns into an inferno at their attack, at their offence against nature. Nature is akin to the god of the Old Testament, on the whole benevolent to the deserving, but ruthless with the undeserving. It is of course the Romantic apotheosis of nature; Owen is using this well-worn poetic tradition more or less unconsciously, both as part of his poetic vocabulary and as an existential framework following his estrangement from orthodox religion. The punitive parent figure cannot easily be left out of the emotional landscape; if that god is ousted, a new one, quickly imbued with similar attributes, is found. In 'Asleep', however, God and nature co-exist in their separate traditional roles, though the whole of the second stanza is an agnostic question: does the dead soldier lie pillowed by God, or does his body merely blend with the 'low mould'?

Who know? Who hopes? Who troubles? Let it pass!
He sleeps. He sleeps less tremulous, less cold
Than we who must awake, and waking, say Alas!

If in Owen's developing agnosticism God is sometimes ousted by the new moral and creative authority of nature, Christ is never specifically relegated. It is a cliché of First World War poetry that the soldiers at the front were sacrificing themselves for others as Christ did on the cross. Owen referred to this idea in his poems until he was posted in France for the second time. In 'At a Calvary near the Ancre' (November 1917) the soldiers are likened to Christ and the church with its army chaplains to the priests and scribes who passed by Christ's sufferings in scorn. The important difference in Owen's use of this analogy is that he uses it as a criticism of the war, 'The scribes . . . brawl allegiance to the state' whereas commonly the analogy was used as a justification of the war. (Compare the war poems of John Oxenham (d.1941), of whose poetry Owen wrote (letter of 10 June 1917) 'the work has little Pacific Value, if you understand me.') The essential difference in Owen's view between Christ and God is shown in 'Soldier's Dream' (October 1917) where 'kind Jesus fouled the big-gun gears . . . and rusted every bayonet with His tears.' But 'God was vexed . . . And . . . he'd seen to our repairs.' God is the Field-Marshal of 'Inspection', and is confused with the authority of the state. Owen's most negative, and final, image of God appears in his letter of Easter Sunday 1918 addressed to his mother:

God so hated the world that He gave several millions of English-begotten sons, that whosoever believeth in them should not perish, but have a comfortable life.

It seems that his rejection of orthodox religion has allowed Owen to use God as a symbol of uncaring authority. (Compare the above passage with the Bible, St John 3.16.) Christ, however, remains as an embodiment of love and the soldiers' link with him is seen in Owen's letter of 16(?) May 1917:

And am I not myself a conscientious objector with a very scared conscience?
  The evangelicals have fled from a few Candles, discreet incense, serene altars, mysterious music, harmonious ritual to powerful electric lighting, overheated atmosphere, palm-tree platforms, grand pianos, loud and animated music, extemporal ritual; but I cannot see that they are any nearer to the Kingdom.
  Christ is literally in no man's land. There men often hear His voice: Greater love hath no man than this, that a man lay down his life—for a friend.

Is it spoken in English only and French?
I do not believe so.
Thus you see how pure Christianity will not fit with pure patriotism.*

The soldiers carry the cross placed on them by the State, or womankind ('Greater Love'), or Owen himself:

> For 14 hours yesterday I was at work—teaching Christ to lift his cross by numbers, and how to adjust his crown; and not to imagine he thirst until after the last halt; I attended his Supper to see that there were no complaints; and inspected his feet to see that they were worthy of the nails. I see to it that he is dumb and stands to attention before his accusers. With a piece of silver I buy him every day, and with maps I make him familiar with the topography of Golgotha. †

It would, however, be quite wrong to suppose that Owen has a consistently developed view of God, Christ, agnosticism and nature. While the soldier is sometimes seen as the Christ-like figure shown in the above examples, this view of the necessity of sacrifice is satirised and rejected in 'Inspection'. God is still benevolent in 'The Parable of the Old Man and the Young'; likewise in 'Asleep', even if his existence is in doubt; and in the first stanza of 'Apologia Pro Poemate Meo' he is a symbol for a transcendent spirit of humanity. On the other hand, in 'Strange Meeting' and 'Spring Offensive', unusually for Owen, the soldiers do not escape accusations. They are sacrificed to no purpose, while being eternally damned for their part in the war. Though Owen maintains, both directly in his choice of theme and indirectly in his empathetic attitude, an overwhelming faith in love and selflessness as symbolised by Christ (and also by the 'negative capability' of Keats), he succumbs at times to despair and confusion. He is himself the embodiment of the irreconcilable conflict of Christianity and patriotism, and he was not the sort of poet who could intellectualise about it with any consistency. There is a revealing passage illustrating this conflict in his letter of 13 August 1917 to his mother:

> Send an English Testament to his Grace of Canterbury, and let it consist of that one sentence, at which he winks his eyes: 'Ye have heard that it *hath* been said "An eye for an eye, and a tooth for a tooth": But I say that ye resist not evil, but whosoever shall smite thee on thy right cheek, turn to him the other also.'
> And if his reply be 'Most unsuitable for the present distressing moment, my dear lady! But I trust that in God's good time . . . etc.'

* *Collected Letters*, p.461.
† Letter to Osbert Sitwell, July 1918. Ibid., p.562.

—then there is only one possible conclusion, that there are no more Christians at the present moment than there were at the end of the first century.

> While I wear my star and eat my rations, I continue to take care of my Other Cheek; and, thinking of the eyes I have seen made sightless, and the bleeding lad's cheeks I have wiped, I say: Vengeance is mine, I, Owen, will repay.

> Let my lords turn to the people when they say 'I believe in... Jesus Christ', and we shall see as dishonest a face as ever turned to the East, bowing, over the Block at Tyburn.*

The nearest Owen comes to a consistent treatment of the dilemma is in his unfailing view of the common soldiers as victims when viewed individually or closely, an obvious outcome of his emotional or empathetic approach to his subjects; but when viewed at a distance they are seen as part of the evil machinery of war. Owen always saw himself as part of that machinery because as an officer he was part of the authority of the state. He is the inspector of 'Inspection', degrading sacrificial blood as 'dirt', he is the head of the corrupting worm in 'The Show' and the murderer of 'Strange Meeting'. The burden and betrayal of authority is a constant theme of his poems, whether revealed in religious imagery or in images of nature.

Other recurring images in his poetry are blood, the heart, and laughter. Blood can be the symbol of guilt, the 'dirt' in 'Inspection' though there it is used with irony. In the same poem it is also the symbol of sacrifice and the beauty of youth. In 'Apologia Pro Poemate Meo' it is the blood-bond of friendship, and the tie with nature in 'Asleep'. In 'Insensibility' the colour of blood is the colour of suffering, and terror has shrunk the soldiers' hearts. Owen's own heart has been rendered small ('The Calls') by his experiences, as he wished for himself in the probably earlier poem 'Insensibility' in order to be able to articulate the horrors of warfare.

In his poetry there is a hint of the sinister in smiles and laughter. The agony of his creative release is accompanied by the gods' laughter and brought about in 'hilarious thunders' in 'Storm' (October 1916). Happiness, laughter and smiles, as in the sonnet 'Three rompers run together' (May 1916) and in 'Sweet is your antique body' (December 1917) have been lost with the loss of innocence ('Happiness', February 1917); in 'Song of Songs' (summer 1917) and 'From My Diary, July 1914' (October 1917), they are an affirmation of life and of love. But in his poem of the same period, 'Has your Soul Sipped?', a smile has the decadent lure of necrophilia. In 'To Eros' (October 1917) laughter is sadistic, and in 'Apologia Pro Poemate Meo' provoked by the absurdity of war. The Virgin in 'Le Christianisme' (November 1917) smiles with evil and

---

* *Collected Letters*, p.483.

seductive intent 'for war to flatter her'. In 'Strange Meeting', the poet knows by the smile of his alter ego that he is in hell. There is the corpse's grin of 'S.I.W.', and the grins of the living corpses in 'Mental Cases':

—Thus their heads wear this hilarious, hideous,
Awful falseness of set-smiling corpses.

In the irony of 'Smile, Smile, Smile' (September 1918)—the title is an allusion to the well known marching song:

What's the use of worrying?
It never was worth while,
So, pack up your troubles in your old kitbag
And smile, smile, smile.

—the only thing to smile about is the peace of death, or worse, the conspiracy of silence over the horrors of the war. In 'Spring Offensive', perhaps the last poem he worked on, Owen ends with the frustrated question about this conspiracy: 'Why speak not they of comrades that went under?' His return to France in 1918 was largely to break this silence:

For leaning out last midnight on my sill
I heard the sighs of men, that have no skill
To speak of their distress, no, nor the will!
    A voice I know. And this time I must go.
                    'The Calls' (May 1918, possibly earlier)

Sound in Owen's poetry

Of his completed poems, there are a dozen or so that use pararhymes. It seems that maybe as early as 1912 Owen noted Shelley's occasional use of pararhyming, but certainly in 1913 on the back of a draft translation of a poem by the Swiss poet Henry Spiess (1876–1940), he listed sequences of pararhymes. His first completed exercise in the use of consonantal rhyming or pararhyming was probably in 'Song of Songs', written in June 1917. Excluding the fragments, a dated list of his pararhymed poems would be as follows, though some of the dates can only be conjectured:

June 1917	'Song of Songs'
July 1917	'Has your Soul Sipped?'
October 1917	'From My Diary, July 1914'
October 1917	'Insensibility'
November 1917	'The Show'
December 1917	'A Terre'
December 1917	'Exposure'
January 1918	'Miners'

January 1918	'Strange Meeting'
February 1918	'The Last Laugh'
May 1918	'Arms and the Boy'
May 1918	'Futility'

The first three non-war poems contain very regular rhyme schemes and the pararhymes tend to be full, that is, both first and end consonants correspond. There is a marked change with the war poem 'Insensibility' where the pararhymes are often more subtle: only the end consonants correspond and some end pararhymes are echoed by internal pararhymes—one a full rhyme; the rhyme scheme is also frequently broken. It is as if his previous more regular experiments had given him the confidence to use this form of rhyming freely for his new subject matter of war. Certainly in this poem the subject largely determines the form of the poem, unlike its three 'aesthetic' pararhymed precursors. After the break marked by 'Insensibility' it becomes hard to generalise about the pararhymed poems. They are all war poems, and some show greater freedom of form than others. Mostly, except for 'The Show', the rhyme-schemes are regular, with only an odd deviation. 'Exposure' displays some of the cleverest full pararhymes—knive us/nervous, silence/non-chalance, snow-dazed/sun-dozed—this last set marking the turning point in the poem. The late date suggested for the very formal and 'aesthetic' poem of 'Futility' is perhaps the most surprising. The rhyme scheme is perfectly regular and each stanza firmly punctuated at its finish with a full rhyme. As with the first three pararhymed poems listed, its content, however, is a good deal less interesting than that of the eight more irregular poems.

Though others before Owen had used this poetic technique, notably Shelley, Keats, and in particular Elizabeth Barrett Browning, Swinburne and Yeats—all of whom Owen had read—he was without question the first poet to use this form of rhyming as sustained and regular end-rhymes in English. (It occurs as a regular internal rhyme scheme in Welsh poetry, but there is no evidence that Owen knew this until Graves mentioned it to him in his letter of December 1917.) This aspect of his work excited quite a lot of interest during his lifetime but especially after his death. It was quickly seen as adding a new flexibility to poetic forms. From the middle of the nineteenth century, poets, especially American ones (notably Emily Dickinson, 1830–86) had experimented with alternatives to full rhymes because of their limiting nature. Many critics have argued that pararhyming is intrinsically discordant and, because of its quality of incompleteness, gives an effect of failure. This, they say, can induce a feeling of hopelessness or despair in the reader. Owen heightens this tendency by sometimes making the second pararhyme lower in pitch than the first, for example, 'groined/groaned', 'grained/ground', 'years/yours', and so on in 'Strange Meeting';

'mean/moan', 'hid/head' in 'The Show'. This lowers and weighs down the sound in a way that can be very melancholic. It is also argued that the sound of pararhymes is somehow dark, muffled or subterranean, fitting for the horrors of trench warfare. Stylistically they do seem to be particularly well suited to colloquial poetry because their unobtrusiveness, as against full rhymes, helps to create an impression of ordinary speech. Of the twelve poems listed, however, at the most two can really be described as belonging to Owen's colloquial genre: 'A Terre', and possibly 'The Last Laugh'. In actual fact, the use of this technique is not easily classifiable. As with onomatopoeia where the appropriateness or imitative nature of the sound of the language must be governed by the meaning of the poem, pararhymes are only melancholic, subterranean and so on, when the context dictates it. The joyfulness of 'On my Songs' and 'From My Diary' clearly illustrates this. In these two cases pararhyming seems to add a sharp, exquisite edge to the sensuousness of the poems (a musical analogy would be the pleasure found in certain discords, for instance in suspended sevenths) and in that respect is particularly appropriate for the decadence of 'Has your Soul Sipped?' where sensuous pleasure is to be found in contemplating a cut throat. Owen had undoubtedly a musical ear and was much concerned with the sound of his poetry. Pararhyming was not confined to end rhyming, but was also much used to internal consonance:

Rucked too thick for these men's extrication

'Mental Cases'

This line also serves to illustrate his highly developed assonance and his evocative use of word sounds that culminate in onomatopoeia:

Only the stuttering rifles' rapid rattle
Can patter out their hasty orisons.

'Anthem for Doomed Youth'

In this poem onomatopoeia is used for the appropriate sounds of mourning so that the whole poem becomes a lament for the dead soldiers. In 'Mental Cases' the denseness and urgency of the language forces facial contortions from the reader that match the anguish of the men 'whose minds the Dead have ravished'. It is as if Owen's pararhyming was an inevitable outcome of his consciousness of sound and his extensive experiments with internal assonance and consonance which had started in his early youth, and which, by his period of 'maturity' (post-Craiglockhart) had become central to the meaning of his poetry. The use of such sensuous devices is associated with love poetry, especially the love poetry of the Romantics, and it imparts to Owen's poetry the quality of a total emotional and physical response to the effects of war. At their best, as in 'Spring Offensive' and 'Mental Cases', these devices help to make the poems powerful and moving.

Part 4

Hints for study

WILFRED OWEN IS NOT AT FIRST SIGHT an easy poet. It takes several readings to understand his borrowed idioms of Romanticism and colloquialism, which are sometimes disconcertingly mixed. He is at times a little obscure; his own half-joking statement to his mother that he was a 'master of elision' is not always true; sometimes he left out too much.

Poetry is intrinsically a dense artistic medium. Each line of verse means more than a first reading indicates. 'Swirled/By the May breeze, murmurous with wasp and midge' (from 'Spring Offensive') does not only mean that the grass was moved by a light wind on a day in May when there were plenty of insects about. The sounds of the line—the alliterations, assonances, onomatopoeia and the rhythm—help to convey the meaning that the day was beautiful and that nature was bountiful. The line also echoes the 'Ode to a Nightingale' of Keats, evoking his view of nature and of man's role so that Owen's own vision is broadened by not being merely set in the present and not merely in circumstances defined by one particular 'offensive' in one particular war. The sensuousness is more than descriptive: nature is not a background to the action of the poem but a protagonist, and is characterised by the poet; sensuousness is an active quality of one of the major participants in the poem. The line also has a distinct ominous quality that is already heralded by the last sentence of the first stanza. This bountiful nature is also the outraged natural law and will wreak her vengeance on the warriors. Thus one randomly picked, seemingly insignificant line has at least five levels of meaning: its simple literal sense, the meaning evoked by its sound, the added meaning of its literary echoes, the meaning that is imparted by its context in the poem so that what could be seen as mere descriptive detail is actually a description of a major protagonist, and, lastly, a tone, a mood of ominousness which is also set by the context. Every line of the poetry should be read bearing in mind this contrapuntal texture. And in order to find and unravel the counterpoint, many readings of each poem are required.

Major aspects of Owen's poetry

As a revision exercise, you should order the poems analysed in these Notes by dates of their first drafts and see what patterns of development you can discern in Owen's writing. You may find the following list of major aspects of his writing useful; you should at any rate be in a position to illustrate *from memory* each of these points before taking an examination, or embarking on any major essay.

(1) The subjects of Owen's pre-Craiglockhart poetry;
(2) Owen's romantic diction;
(3) the major literary influences on his early work;
(4) the effect of his stay at Craiglockhart and his meeting with Sassoon; the new influences on his work;
(5) Owen's pararhyming;
(6) the development of his attitude towards the war, its victims and its survivors;
(7) Owen's Preface and Table of Contents: his war poetry as elegiac, the extent of his rejection of 'aesthetic' poetry;
(8) his view of God, Christ and nature;
(9) his view of authority and of the 'Two Nations';
(10) his concern with his own conflicting roles as poet and decrier of war, and soldier and murderer;
(11) the light thrown on his poems by passages from his letters;
(12) recurring images in his poetry.

All these points have been illustrated and discussed in these Notes. You should now draw them together in a tabular form, expanding and improving upon the comments on each aspect of Owen's work if you can.

Examination essays

If you have a choice, choose a question which interests you. Genuine interest in an answer always tells, making the essay more attractive for the reader or examiner. Always stick to the question; do not write down everything you know about Owen or the poem(s)—this is never required. You will be expected to show that you can organise what you know for a specific purpose or topic and that you can pick out what is relevant from your knowledge. Always make notes first and organise your notes into a clear argument before you start writing. This is time well spent in an examination. The very act of note-making and organising clears your thoughts and develops coherent arguments in your mind. This is the stage when you must make sure everything you are going to include in your essay is *relevant to the essay topic*.

You should illustrate every major point in your essay with suitable quotations. This shows close acquaintance with the texts, which is what the examiner is looking for. It also keeps your arguments strictly to the evidence of the text and again, examiners look for this approach. The wise student finds significant passages in the set works, illustrating the major aspects of the author's works and learns them by heart before the examination. In the case of Owen, some passages from his letters should be learnt as well. (The most significant passages from the letters are quoted in these Notes.) You should match the list of major aspects of his work on page 75 with relevant quotations which you should then write out and learn.

In the examination room, when you have jotted down your ideas on the set topic in note form, arrange them into a sequence of paragraphs, cutting out repetitions and checking that there is a logical development in your arguments. This planning stage is the most important part of answering the question even though you have not yet written down anything for the examiner. Allow about one quarter of your set time for each answer for this procedure. If you have one hour in which to answer a question, you can spend up to fifteen minutes on the planning. This is time well spent, and for most examinations you can submit your essay plan to the examiner with your written-out answer which should include apt quotations illustrating and proving your major points.

When you embark on the writing of your essay, try to start each of your paragraphs with a clear statement of the paragraph topic so that your essay does not degenerate into a long list of directionless information about the author and his works. Having made a good plan, stick to it. When you reach the end of your arguments, sum up your essay in a concluding paragraph. This should draw together your preceding arguments and should not normally introduce any major new idea.

Do not spend more than the time allotted on any one essay, time yourself ruthlessly on each question so that you are able to make an attempt on all the required answers. You cannot make up for almost total ignorance in one section of the examination by spending much more time on the questions you feel able to answer well.

Sample examination essays

Here are two sample essays on two major aspects of Owen's work. They are just under a thousand words in length, the averge for examination essays written in less than an hour.

'Above all I am not concerned with Poetry.' How true do you find this statement of Owen's? Discuss with reference to his war poetry.

This essay topic is inviting you to consider what Owen meant by 'Poetry' in his quotation, hence some discussion of the Preface is called for. His war poems will then have to be set against his idea of 'Poetry'. Varying emphasis can be given to the form and content (ideas) of the poems—there is no right answer in this respect. The ability to make a good job of this essay depends very much on the analysis of the quotation and an understanding of one of the dichotomies underlying Owen's work, that of propagandist versus poet.

A suggested essay plan

Part 1: Origin of quotation:
The Preface and its meaning.

How Owen saw his role as a poet:
poetic craftsman and spokesman for soldiers, 'The Poetry is in the pity'.

Part 2: The 'poeticisms' of his war poetry:
colloquial idiom, for instance 'The Dead-Beat'
romantic idiom, for instance 'Hospital Barge'

Emotional force given to his messages by poetic devices, for instance 'Anthem for Doomed Youth'.

Deliberate breaking of poetic conventions, giving shock effect and greater naturalism:
Irregularity of metre
rhyme
pararhyming
for instance 'Exposure', 'A Terre', 'Disabled'.

'Apologia Pro Poemate Meo': measure of the romantic world meeting with modern world; has bitterest expression in 'Greater Love'

Part 3: (Conclusion)
War brings new set of values, shocks Owen out of poetic reveries, gives moral purpose,
former idioms now inadequate,
'Poetry' is term he used for the idiom of his nineteenth-century 'aesthetic' mentors.

Joint development of Owen's moral view and his poetic craftsmanship.

The quotation is taken from Owen's Preface to his intended volume of war poems which was to have been published in 1919. The Preface, though much revised by Owen, was unfinished and contains many ambiguities. The general impression that it leaves is of an intense but barely articulated anger about current attitudes towards the war as evinced in popular poetry and the press. However, Owen does not dare to criticise these attitudes directly; his explanations of his own attitudes in his poems are as much criticism as he allows himself. By 'Poetry' he seems to mean 'poetry for its own sake', that is, the poetry of the nineteenth-century aesthetic school. In his war poems, poetry is for him the means of informing his readers of the truth of war, of arousing pity: 'My subject is War, and the pity of War.' His experiences at the front had convinced him that he had a role of 'watching their suffering that I may speak of them as well as a pleader can'. The importance of the new subject of war had led him to reject the subject matter of much pre-war poetry, as 'Greater Love' and 'Apologia Pro Poemate Meo' reveal. But, on the other hand, there is no evidence that he became uninterested in the craft of poesy because of the war; quite the contrary. His major contributions to twentieth-century poetic form, that of pararhyming, was very largely developed in his war poems.

Owen's war poetry is expressed in two contrasting idioms: that of the Romantic poetry of the previous century used by him throughout his short life as a poet, and that of a more realistic and colloquial style learnt from Siegfried Sassoon in mid-1917. Both of course show a concern for the effectiveness of his poetic expression, and his later war poems begin to show an individual voice synthesised from these two styles. The earlier colloquialisms of, for example, '"That scum you sent last night soon died. Hooray!"' (from 'The Dead-Beat', summer 1917) and the romance of 'Hospital Barge at Cérisy' (December 1917) are united in 'Spring Offensive' (July 1918) in a timeless and universal view of the iniquity of war, arresting in its realism and intense in its romantic emotionalism:

> For though the summer oozed into their veins
> Like an injected drug for their bodies' pains,
> Sharp on their souls hung the imminent line of grass,
> Fearfully flashed the sky's mysterious glass.

In 'Anthem for Doomed Youth' (autumn 1917) poetic devices found in Owen's Romantic models, such as onomatopoeia and alliteration, are used to great effect, adding to the emotional intensity of the poem:

> Only the stuttering rifles' rapid rattle
> Can patter out their hasty orisons.

Internal pararhyming is used to imitate the echo of returning gun fire, for example, 'Only the monstrous anger of the guns', and sensuous alliterations and assonances of the sonnet's contrasting sestet underline the strength of the emotions of mourning felt by the relatives of the doomed youths. His consciousness of poetic devices and his increasingly confident handling of them are seen in his deliberate breaking of established practices: irregularity of metre and freedom in stanza length lend naturalism to speech as in 'Disabled' and 'A Terre'. In 'Exposure' inverted feet and anapaestic substitutions give some lines an effect of stumbling, adding an aural dimension to the image of the foundering soldiers:

Northward, incessantly, the flickering gunnery rumbles
Far off, like a dull rumour of some other war.

The certainty of perfect rhyming is interrupted by pararhymes to build up the pervading tone of insecurity and anxiety, for instance, 'silence/ nonchalance'. Though all his war poems embody aesthetic poeticisms, many used to great effect, the meeting of the romantic world with the harsher realities of the modern world is shown most clearly in 'Greater Love' and 'Apologia Pro Poemate Meo' where each poem is constructed on the ironies which arise when traditional honorific terms are applied to soldiers battling in the trenches:

I have perceived much beauty
In the hoarse oaths that kept our courage straight

and

Red lips are not so red
As the stained stones kissed by the English dead.

The war and Owen's encounter with Sassoon brought a new set of values to his poetry. He was shocked out of his self-indulgent and imitative writing by finding a moral purpose, that of voicing the sufferings of the common soldier. In order to do so effectively, he expanded his romantic style by sporadically adopting a more naturalistic idiom and by refining his use of poetic devices to, in places, virtuoso perfection. 'Exposure' (begun December 1917, finished September 1918) and 'Spring Offensive' (July-September 1918) are the outstanding products of this process. Now that Jon Stallworthy has produced the most reliable chronology of Owen's poems to date, it is possible to say that his moral view developed jointly with his poetic craftsmanship, culminating in the morally intense and aesthetically polished poems of his last six months. Only in the sense that Owen rejected poetry for its own sake can it be said that he was 'not concerned with Poetry'.

'We make out of the quarrel with others rhetoric but out of the quarrel with ourselves poetry' (W.B. Yeats). How true is this in relation to Wilfred Owen's poetry?

This essay hinges on a good understanding of the term rhetoric, against which Owen's poems can then be measured, and on knowing which of his poems are self-questioning in nature. For a short essay only the most outstanding examples from the poems should be used. As in the first essay, an understanding of one of the major dichotomies in his work is called for, but this time the emphasis is on Owen being both a perpetrator (as soldier) and decrier (as poet) of the war.

A suggested essay plan
Part 1:   (Introduction)
              Definition of rhetoric.
              Two major aspects of Owen's work revealed in Preface:
                   anti-war propaganda (rhetoric)
                   elegiac writing (poetry)

Part 2:   Rhetoric of juvenilia:
              'O World of Many Worlds'
              'On My Songs"
              '1914'
              Rhetoric of indignation:
              'The Dead-Beat'
              'Dulce Et Decorum Est'
              Rhetoric of aestheticism:
              'Futility'

Part 3:   Poetry of self-questioning:
              'Inspection'
              'Asleep'
              ('The Shows')
              'Strange Meeting'
              'Spring Offensive'

Part 4   (Conclusion) Necessary role of rhetoric

Rhetoric is the art of influencing in speech or writing the thought and behaviour of an audience. It contains an intrinsic tendency to emphasise the ends rather than the means. If the means is an art form, such as poetry, it may well be devalued by the urgency of the purpose and degenerate into bombast, or hyperbole. It may furthermore be the means by which too much attention is drawn to the speaker or writer rather than to the quality of his thought, as rhetoric is often a vehicle used in the pursuit of power. Yeats's perceptive statement made about poetry in general in *Anima Hominis* (1917) is particularly relevant to the works of Wilfred Owen. The somewhat evasive contents of Owen's Preface show a dichotomy in his poetry. On the one hand there is an urgency to reveal the horrors of war, and an ill-suppressed wish to stir his readers to some kind of action through his warnings and implied criticisms:

> This book is not about heroes . . . Nor is it about deeds, or lands, nor anything about glory, honour, might, majesty, dominion or power, except War.

On the other hand, there is a stress on pity and on the elegiac nature of his writing:

My subject is War, and the pity of War.
The Poetry is in the pity.
Yet these elegies are to this generation in no sense consolatory.

The mode of indignation inspires action while that of the elegy inspires pity. Owen was both an anti-war propagandist, and as such a rhetorician and lesser poet, and a writer of elegies produced by the profound pity emanating from his irreconcilable role of critic (poet) of the war and soldier (murderer) in the war, which, together with his polished craftsmanship, has earned him a prominent place in the history of poetry.

In his juvenilia there is a self-consciousness and posturing that could be labelled as rhetorical, in so far as it draws attention to himself and his role as a poet, rather than to the merit of his art alone, particularly in 'O World of many Worlds' and to a lesser extent in 'On My Songs'. By '1914' it is translated into a grandiose posturing which is an attempt to convey the momentous historical import of the outbreak of the war. In it, there are moments of artistic success; the subject dominates rather than the poet's awareness of the reader. In 1917, however, when first-hand experience of trench warfare and Owen's encounter with the maturer Siegfried Sassoon had convinced him of the futility and evil of the war, an entirely new set of attitudes developed in his poetry.

His stance is seen most clearly in the poems of undiluted indignation against the war. 'The Dead-Beat' quarrels with 'all the valient, that aren't dead:/Bold uncles' and the doctor and stretcher-bearers who are safe behind the lines of battle. The indignation, if not hatred, spills over onto the anti-hero subject who 'Lay stupid like a cod', so that the poem is saturated in a disgust and bitterness that leaves little scope for the reader to form his own judgments. Written in the same colloquial style, 'The Letter', by its sympathetic portrayal of a soldier writing home to his wife while under fire, evokes a far stronger response against the war in the reader. The former poem is closer to rhetoric, the latter to poetry. 'Dulce Et Decorum Est' where he quarrels with the patriotic poet and writer for children, Jessie Pope and others of her kind:

If you could hear . . .
My friend, you would not tell with such high zest
To children ardent for some desperate glory,
The Old Lie

contains rhetorical hyperbole in its unrelieved descriptions of battle-field horror:

All went lame; all blind;
Drunk with fatigue; deaf even . . .

but is sometimes redeemed as poetry in vivid patches of apt description:

An esctasy of fumbling . . .
Dim, through the misty panes and thick green light,
As under a green sea, I saw him drowning.

'Futility' descends to rhetorical posturing in its quarrel with the sun,
the symbol of the life-force, which in this poem seems to become responsible for death in war. Here Owen has been too interested in the
form, which is finely crafted rhythmically and in its rhyme schemes, to
allow for a morally sound view of the subject matter. It is an aesthetic
posturing in front of his readers.

When Owen questions his own role in the war, however, or 'quarrels
with himself' in the search for truth, his finest poems are wrought.
'Inspection' (August 1917) is among the first of these. In it, Owen is
both a perpetrator of the war as one of its officers and the poet who
exposes the hypocrisies of war. The blood that must be white-washed
away is a symbol of the realities of war, its guilt and suffering, as well
as of the life and innocence of the soldiers. While being realistic, it
avoids over-emphasis on horror or suffering and in its witty irony
which contrasts army ritual with that of religion, it allows readers to
draw their own conclusions about the nature of war. The calm, plain
writing of 'Asleep' puts forward the question: what life after death? in
the terrible context of the war:

He sleeps. He sleeps less tremulous, less cold
Than we who must awake, and waking, say Alas!

There is no quarrel in the poem, only an acceptance of suffering and
futility: 'Who knows? Who hopes? Who troubles? Let it pass!'

Though the horror of 'The Show' incorporates a realisation of the
poet's own role in the war, it is unable to match the richness and com-
plexity with which this theme is treated in 'Strange Meeting'. Here the
poet meets his *alter ego* in the profundity of his dreams, the soldier
poet from the enemy's side. This *Doppelgänger*, a theme with countless
literary precedents appropriate to its universal significance and Owen's
dichotomous position, reveals the consequences of Owen's involvement with the war as well as the war's impact on mankind. The waste
of life and talent, the silencing of truth, the emergence of totalitarian-
ism are all shown to be the outcome:

Now men will go content with what we spoiled
Or, discontent, boil bloody, and be spilled.
They will be swift with swiftness of the tigress.
None will break ranks, though nations trek from progress.

But art is seen as the redeeming force, cleansing with truth the blood-
clogged chariot wheels. The poem dramatises the irresolvable conflict

of Owen's life as both a soldier and poet, and quarrels with no-one but himself: 'I am the enemy you killed, my friend.'

The culmination of his self-questioning is reached in what was probably his last poem, 'Spring Offensive'. Here it is transferred away from himself onto the conscience of other soldiers: 'Why speak not they of comrades that went under?' For Owen had made it his business to speak of those 'that went under' in for example, 'The Sentry', 'Mental Cases', 'A Terre', and 'S.I.W.'.

However, before condemning 'The Dead-Beat', 'Dulce Et Decorum Est', 'Futility', as rhetoric, it should be borne in mind that Owen died at the age of twenty-five, survived by no more than 110 completed poems. In so far as rhetoric is the study of effective use of language it is a necessary part of a poet's growth, even if it brings vanity or hyperbole in its train. The profundity of thought in 'Strange Meeting' with its mastery of poetic form and innovatory pararhyming could not have been achieved without self-conscious experimentation with language or without Owen convincing himself that he was a poet by toying with the idea of adopting that role. Owen's voice remained part of the self-conscious romantic literary tradition which he echoed in 'Strange Meeting', stretching from Dante to Shelley, Keats, Wilde and Barbusse, and which is concerned with the aesthetic or rhetorical use of language.

Additional essay topics

Here are two more essay topics with some suggested approaches:

(1) Compare and contrast views of nature in two of Owen's poems.

Choose examples that are clearly contrasting. '1914' and 'Spring Offensive' would be a good choice, or 'From My Diary, July 1914' and 'Exposure'. Nature in Owen's work has several faces (see Part 3, p.66–7): it is the source of aesthetic joys, the cycle of life; it is ravaged and degraded by war and therefore takes vengeance. Remember too that nature takes the place of God in some of Owen's poems. A suggested plan for this essay would be:

An Introduction discussing briefly Owen's view of nature in general

The substance of the essay containing a comparison of your choice of poems showing how they each reveal aspects of Owen's view of nature

Chronology, that is, their placing in the development of Owen's work will be important

Do not discuss one poem on its own and then the other. It is better to make comparisons throughout. This will require some planning at the note-making stage. *The conclusion* should pick out the major comparisons and show if they reveal any major developments in Owen's thinking, for example his adoption of nature as a substitute for God.

By what means did Owen try to convey the horrors of war in his poetry?

For this question you will have to do a quick survey of all Owen's war poems. You may come up with the following pattern:

(i) Initial grandiose vision, 'On seeing a piece of our heavy artillery' and '1914', soon replaced by fear of death, by no hope in the afterlife in 'The Unreturning' and 'The End', and by a realisation of the permanent corrupting nature of certain experiences, as shown in 'Happiness'.

(ii) Moves to a unique concern with the mutilated survivors of war, as 'Disabled', 'Conscious', 'A Terre', 'Mental Cases', 'The Sentry'.

(iii) In 'Greater Love' contrasts the old values with the new reality. The horror is high-lighted by the new use to which the devices of Romantic poetry are put. Sensuousness of romantic idiom used to enforce his message: 'Anthem for Doomed Youth'.

(iv) New realism in writing, for instance, 'The Dead-Beat', 'The Letter', 'The Sentry', gives an immediacy to his writing.

(v) Uses religion to illustrate the betrayal of the young by the old as in 'Parable of the Old Man and the Young', and to show that the sin of pride as well as sexual vanity is behind the war ('Le Christianisme').

(vi) Culmination of his portrayal of war is in the intensely personal vision and idiom (a mixture of the Romantic idiom and modern colloquialisms) of 'Strange Meeting' and 'Spring Offensive' where the reader is moved by Owen's inability to reconcile his roles of poet and soldier.

Quotations from the poems should illsutrate each point made.

Essay titles for further practice

(1) Which of the poems of Owen do you consider to be his best and why?
(2) 'He [Owen] is all blood, dirt and sucked sugar stick' (W.B. Yeats). Do you agree with this statement? Discuss with reference to three of Owen's poems.
(3) 'Passive suffering is not a theme for poetry' (W.B. Yeats). Do you think that Owen's poetry is concerned with passive suffering? Discuss with close reference to his poems.

(4) Had Owen developed a poetic voice of his own before his death? Illustrate your answer with close reference to his poems.

(5) Compare and contrast views of religion in two of Owen's poems.

(6) How did Owen see his role as a poet during the war?

Part 5

Suggestions for further reading

Editions of the *Poems*

BLUNDEN, EDMUND (ED.): *The Poems of Wilfred Owen*, Chatto and Windus, London, first published 1931, with many subsequent reprints and editions. Contains Blunden's memoir of Owen, a few notes and, in the appendix, a brief memoir by Frank Nicholson. This is the first lengthy edition of Owen's poetry; the collection contains fifty-nine poems while Siegfried Sassoon's 1920 edition has only twenty-three.

DAY LEWIS, C. (ED.): *The Collected Poems of Wilfred Owen*, Chatto and Windus, London, first published in 1963 with numerous reprints. Contains Introduction and Notes by C. Day Lewis, and a reprint of Edmund Blunden's memoir of his 1931 edition of the poems. Lewis's edition contains eighty poems, including nearly all of the war poetry.

HIBBERD, DOMINIC (ED.): *Wilfred Owen: War Poems and Others*, Chatto and Windus, London first published in 1973. Contains fifty-six poems and an introduction and notes by Hibberd, the most inspired and incisive of Owen's editors.

STALLWORTHY, JON (ED.): *The Complete Poems of Wilfred Owen*, Volume I: The Poems; Volume II: The Manuscripts, Chatto and Windus, London, 1983. This complete edition includes all known poems by Owen in chronological sequence and in their final form. All variants are recorded and the two-volume format allows poems and manuscripts to be consulted together.

Memoirs and biography

OWEN, HAROLD: *Journey from Obscurity: Wilfred Owen 1893–1918: Memoirs of the Owen Family*, Oxford University Press, London, 3 vols, 1963–5. A lengthy and sympathetic account of the Owen family's struggle to make their way in life, written by Wilfred's brother.

STALLWORTHY, JON: *Wilfred Owen: A Biography*, Oxford University Press, London, 1974; paperback, 1977. The first full biography of

Wilfred Owen, drawing heavily on Harold Owen's three volumes, and on the *Collected Letters* (see below). A disappointing work despite (or perhaps because of) the indiscriminatory mass of information collected in its three hundred pages. Its chief value lies in its appendices: one listing the books in Wilfred Owen's possession, now housed in the English Faculty Library at Oxford.

Letters

OWEN, HAROLD and BELL, JOHN (EDS.): *Wilfred Owen: Collected Letters*, Oxford University Press, London, 1967. Alas, some original letters have been irrevocably censored by Harold Owen, but nevertheless the book contains the known total of Wilfred Owen's letters (673) most of which are addressed to his mother, Susan Owen. A few can be read as preludes to his war poems and show that specific incidents were often his inspiration.

Biographical and critical studies

BÄCKMAN, SVEN: *Tradition Transformed: Studies in the poetry of Wilfred Owen*, C.W.K. Gleerup, Lund, 1979, The most up-to-date monograph on Owen's poetry, throwing much light on the literary origins of his writing, its musical references, and his use of pararhyme.

HIBBERD, DOMINIC: *Wilfred Owen* (Writers and Their Work series, British Council), Longman, London, 1975. A short work of less than forty pages that nevertheless contains more critical insights and a clearer outline of Owen's life and works than can easily be distilled from the unfocused detail of Stallworthy's biography. Contains a dated list of Owen's poems, now superseded in one or two instances by Stallworthy's complete edition of the poems.

McILROY, JAMES F.: *Wilfred Owen's Poetry: a study guide*, Heinemann Educational, London, 1974. Commonsense analyses of Owen's major war poems.

PRESS, JOHN: *A Map of Modern English Verse*, Oxford University Press, London, 1969. An introduction to English poetry of the first half of the twentieth century. It is an annotated and copiously explained anthology with an introduction to each section and brief bibliographies of each poet. Owen appears in a section on Poets of the First World War with four of his poems. Good background reading, giving a clear view of Owen's place among these two or three generations of poets.

WELLAND, D.S.R.: *Wilfred Owen: A Critical Study*, Chatto and Windus, London, 1960. The first monograph on Owen's poetry to be published. Contains invaluable judgements and information. For the purposes of the readers of these Notes, Chapters III (The Impact of the War on Owen's poetry) and VI (Half-rhyme) would probably be the most useful. Welland's discussion of the poems' chronology has been superseded by Stallworthy's work.

WHITE, GERTRUDE M.: *Wilfred Owen*, Twayne Publishers Inc., New York, 1969. A short (150 pages), clear, if somewhat adulatory, account of Owen's growth as a poet, now sometimes superseded by later research not yet incorporated in an up-to-date critical study of Owen. Still remains therefore a valuable piece of background reading.

The author of these notes

BENEDIKTE UTTENTHAL was born in Denmark and educated in England where she took degrees at the Universities of Cambridge and Essex. She worked for several years at the Open University headquarters in Milton Keynes and then moved into the fields of Adult and Further Education. She is currently working in Scotland as the Education Officer of a penal institution. This is her second *York Note*, the first being on Tom Stoppard's *Professional Foul*.